Elements

The visual building blocks.

Graeme Smith

PUBLISHED ON AMAZON.com
by
LABYRINTH BOOKS

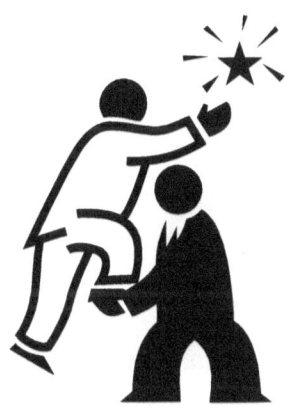

DEDICATION:

This book is dedicated to my family.
    Hele-ly (Ly).
          my wife:

    Ingrid.
          our daughter:

    Marie.
          my former wife:

    Fiona, Natalie and Michael
          our children:

    Georgie
          Michael's wife:

    Pearl, Kiki and Martha.
          their children:

They have put up with me for many years and I thank them for that.
I hope this book gives an insight into what occupied me much of the time.
All have done worthwhile and interesting things without my help.
I congratulate them for their achievements.

SUPPORT:

Support the International Artist magazine –
contact: editor@internationalartist.com

Support the Australian Artist magazine –
contact: editor@australianartist.com

HOW TO USE THIS BOOK.

People don't think through things to a level they need to.
Because of that, they have projects instead of tasks on a "to do" list.
That leads to procrastination as it hasn't been broken to a task level.
Go through your book once to understand it then go through it again.
Start at the **PART** of the book that you think you should start at.
Make notes of steps you will need to take and the resources required.
Use the notes to make a step by step system to implement the ideas.
Often you won't refer to the original, you've created YOUR system.

A first question to ask and answer is "Why is this being done?"
How does this align with where you want to get to?
What are the strategic implications of doing this?
Does this fit with getting to your goal in the shortest and fastest time?
What would it be like if it were totally successful?
Define it - what is success for this project and how will you know?

Now brainstorm all the tasks are involved.
It's important not to go linear too fast, so step one, two, and step four.
Otherwise you end up cutting off options.
As you plan one, two, three, there's a specific step that might be four.
Start steps too quickly, other ways of doing them may not appear.

The first third of a brainstorming session is easy, generate ideas.
The second third is a little bit more challenging.
Go through those ideas and see where they lead to.
Push yourself to think a bit outside the box that's where a big idea is!
The most powerful way of getting a project done fastest is there.

Most people never get to that level.
They end up short-changing themselves.
Then a project takes longer and they also tend to procrastinate.
This final brainstorming part of the equation is incredibly important.

INDEX: ELEMENTS and PRINCIPLES.

1. VISUAL RELATIONSHIPS.

2. DEPTH:

3. LIGHT:

1. VISUAL RELATIONSHIPS.

There is NO visual thing with only one element.
      1. EVERYTHING has more or less of all of them.
      2. What relationships do aesthetic principles refer to?
      3. Elements include:

1. EVERYTHING has more or less of all of them.

Visual elements are thus concepts when considered independently.
But in reality they do not happen like that.

Reality is the relationship between various visual elements in a thing.
The focus here is on Tone, Texture, Colour and Shape.

Visual element: Tone (or value)
The factor that indicates darkness or lightness or light and shade.
Tones may vary between extreme dark (black) and extreme light (white).
These intermediate tones are grey.

Visual element: Colour
Colours are often grouped according to their mixing properties.
Primary colours (red, blue, yellow) cannot be made by mixing other colours.
Secondary colours are made by mixing two primary colours.
Green – yellow and blue; orange – yellow and red; purple – blue and red.
Tertiary colours such as brown, grey, rust are mixtures of all primary colours.
Tints such (pink) are mixtures where white is one colour.
A shade (olive) is a colour mixed with black or a darker colour.

Visual element: Texture
The factor that indicates tactile quality of a surface.
Texture may be rough or smooth, gritty or greasy, etc.
Texture may be actual (sandpaper) or implied but it is still visual.

Visual element: Shape
The factor that indicates external form.
That which shape encloses is area.
Shapes may be simple such as square, triangle, circle, oval or rectangle.
But they can also be complex such as an eye.

Visual element: Line

The factor that indicates a row, series, course or contour.

Line may be strokes or long narrow marks.

Line may be straight, curved, broken, jagged, flowing or a combination.

Line has length and breadth where length is dominant.

It can be thick or thin and has direction.

A series of lines if joined, shape, area and space may be defined by the line.

Line is two-dimensional (flat pencil lines) but can be three-dimensional (wire).

Visual element: Size

The factor that indicates dimension.

Size may be large, small, of somewhere in between.

Visual element: Mass

The factor that indicates heavy or light weight, or density or solidity of matter.

Simple forms of mass are sphere, cone, cube, pyramid, prism, or ovoid.

Mass relates to space and may be real (lump of clay) or apparent (drawn).

Visual element: Space

Space relates to a lack of obvious other element (particularly mass and line).

However space usually relates to being inside, outside, under or over.

Space may be open (incomplete) or closed (a boundary).

Space also may be actual or implied.

It is sometimes termed environment.

Visual element: Direction

The factor that indicates aim or course of movement.

The movement may be actual or suggested.

Direction may be horizontal, vertical or oblique and relates to a plane or axis.

There is a start and an end and can be seen in a serial order or sequence.

2. What relationships do aesthetic principles refer to?

With visual material the elements are obviously visual (see above).
If an aesthetic material was a sound a different set of elements would apply.
This is one way music is different from art.

The visual elements are combined in a range of relationships.
Those relationships are the aesthetic principles.
Even other aesthetic material has the same set of relationships (sounds).

In art the elements are visual and so too are the principles.
In music this would not be the case.

Aesthetic principles are thus ways the different elements are organized.
It's about how the parts are related to the whole.

The aesthetic principles are concepts which concern relationships.
There may be many such relationships in any visual material.
Aesthetic principles are the relationship of various aspects of an element to the totality of that element within the visual material (image, painting, flower).

Aesthetic principle: Harmony
Concerns agreement, closeness, relatedness or similarity of parts.
The parts may be related through common use (biro and pencil).
They might share aspects of an element (red orange and brown colours).

Aesthetic principle: Contrast
Concerns dissimilar parts within an element (black and white tones).
Discord is extreme contrast (pale pink and orange).
Major contrast is obvious (black and white).
Minor contrast is where there is little difference (dark grey and brown).
Variety may be created by using contrast.

Aesthetic principle: Rhythm

Movement, regular measured beat, flow, throb, pulsation in an element.

Rhythm is repetition, gradation, alteration, radiation sequence (many marks).

Exact repetition can lead to monotony.

Rhythm is related to direction.

The movement may be actual or implied.

Aesthetic principle: Emphasis

Concerns vigour, or stress on important parts.

Emphasis of an element aspect at the expense of another is dominance.

Emphasis may be by using contrast, radiation, majority area, or repetition.

Aesthetic principle: Unity

Concerns cohesion, integration, standardization or singleness of the parts.

Unity adds wholeness to a work.

Unity may come from one aspect being dominant, joining aspects into a combination, enclosing a border, repetition or adding one aspect to the rest.

Add white to other colours, and materials.

Aesthetic principle: Balance

Concerns equilibrium, stability or arrangement of parts within an element.

Balance may be symmetric (equal about an axis), radiate (from a point) or asymmetric (informal).

A paper folded in the centre is symmetric.

Balance may be actual or implied.

Aesthetic principle: Proportion

Concerns quantity, or share of parts within an element.

Proportion is a comparison of parts.

Some parts may be dominant or subsidiary.

3. Elements include:

TONE (or Value):

An illusion of distance can be created by how you use tone (value).
Employing dark and light is a basic element for realism in painting (anything).

Tone (or Value) indicates darkness or lightness or light and shade.
May vary from extreme dark (black) to extreme light (white).
These intermediate tones are grey.

Tone is present in other elements.
Colours possess tone in that they are lighter or darker than other colours.
Lines can be thick or thin and thus show tonal variations.

Tone combines with other elements according to aesthetic principles.
Harmonious areas can combine to form a larger tonal area.
Tones may contrast (black and white) or be similar (different blues)
Repetition of tonal areas creates rhythm.
Tonal emphasis may use contrast, radiation, majority area, or repetition.
Join aspects to a combination unity adds wholeness one aspect dominant.
Tonal balance is symmetric (on axis), radiate (from point) or asymmetric.
Some tonal parts may be dominant or subsidiary.

TEXTURE.

An illusion of distance can be created by texture.
Using various textures to do this is a basic element for realism in painting.

Texture is the factor that indicates tactile quality of a surface.
Texture may be rough or smooth, gritty or greasy, etc.
Textures vary between extreme roughness and extreme smoothness.
There are intermediate textures.

Texture is present in other elements.
Texture may be actual (sandpaper) or implied but still visual.
Lines can be combined as textural variations.

Based on aesthetic principles texture combines with other elements.
Textures may be dominant or subsidiary.
Harmonious areas can combine to form a larger textural area.
Textures may contrast (rough and smooth) or be similar (different fur)
Repetition of texture creates rhythm.
Use contrast, radiation, majority area, or repetition to emphasize texture.
Textural unity adds wholeness: A part dominant, or joined as combination,
Textural balance: Symmetric (equal on axis), radiate (from point) asymmetric.

COLOUR.

An illusion of distance can be created by how you use colour.
Use colour to do this is a basic element of realism in painting anything.

Colours indicates hue and are grouped according to mixing properties.
Primary colours (red, blue, yellow) cannot be made by mixing other colours.
Secondary colours are made by mixing two primary colours.
Tertiary colours: brown, grey, rust are mixtures of the primary colours.

Colour is present in other elements.
Tints such as pink are tonal mixtures where white is one colour.
A shade (olive) is a colour mixed with black or a darker colour.

Colour combines with other elements according to aesthetic principles.
Harmonious areas can combine to form a larger coloured area.
Colours may contrast (red and green) or be similar (red and orange)
Repetition of colour creates rhythm.
Use contrast, radiation, majority area, or repetition to emphasize colour.
Colour unity adds wholeness: If aspect dominant, or joined as a combination,
Colour balance is symmetric (on axis), radiate (from a point) or asymmetric.
Colours may be dominant or subsidiary.

SHAPE.

An illusion of distance can be created by how you use shape.
Using shapes to do this is a basic element for realism in painting (anything).

Shape is the factor that indicates external form.
That which shape encloses is area.
Shapes may be simple such as square, triangle, circle, oval or rectangle.
But they can also be complex such as an eye.
Varying shapes between extremely precise and extremely blurred.
There are intermediate shapes.

Shape is present in other elements.
Lines can be combined as shapes variations.
Colour has area which is a shape.

Shape combines with other elements according to aesthetic principles.
Harmonious areas can combine to form larger areas.
Shapes may contrast (big and small) or be similar.
Repetition of shape creates rhythm.
Use contrast, radiation, majority area, or repetition for emphasis of shape.
Shape unity adds wholeness: One aspect dominant, or joined in combination,
Shape balance symmetric (equal on axis), radiate (from point) or asymmetric.

2. DEPTH:

1. START: TONAL DEPTH Use an experimental attitude.
2. START: TEXTURAL DEPTH
3. START: COLOUR DEPTH
4. START: SHAPE DEPTH

Use an experimental attitude.

Let's see what happens here when I do this?
But be scientific about your art learning too.
Set yourself challenges.

This program isn't about producing instant pictures.
In fact this part of the program isn't about pictures at all!
This program is on learning something about tone and depth.

This program is about doing.
There's no other way.

In this program learn simple things and gradually combine them.
You learn some very complex things that way too.

If paint is used then only a minimum quantity is necessary.
Limited materials will encourage more thoughtful responses.
Creativity, an ability to do most with least, is developed.

In science the task of combining many variables is highly skilled.
So repeat an element rather than use too many different ones.

Don't worry about whether you are doing the experiments correctly.
Do something and it's just about certain to be right.
In the process you'll discover whatever you find out.

Most importantly the discoveries are yours.

They are part of your actual experience rather than following instructions.

Your knowledge grows from your own experiences.

This is what real learning is about.

Take your time.

Don't rush enjoy the experience and see what you can find out.

Fluency comes with practice so be persistent.

1. START: TONAL DEPTH

FIRST Experience Unit:

UNIT 1: Experiment 1
Photocopy or print out the image you have chosen.
Modify size to maintain conformity with your Magic Multiple Miniatures.

Rule or draw a horizontal line across your selected pattern.
The pattern could be either horizontal or vertical (you choose).
The line could be ruled straight or drawn freely.
The line could even follow contours created by the shapes in your pattern.
The horizontal line represents the most distant part of your pattern.
Materials:
Very small amounts of black and white paint.
A brush.
A pattern with a horizontal line.
Begin:
Paint over the pattern.
Try to add depth to the pattern using just tonal variation (dark and light).

UNIT 1: Experiment 2

Photocopy or print the image you used in the previous experiment.

Rule or draw a horizontal line across your selected pattern.

The pattern could be either horizontal or vertical (you choose).

The horizontal line represents the most distant part of your pattern.

Materials:

Very small amounts of black and white paint.

Two different sized brushes.

A pattern with a horizontal line.

Begin:

Use different combinations (black, gray, white) than previous experiment.

Paint over the pattern.

Try to add depth to the pattern using just tonal variations.

Initially draw with the brush and thin paint.

Then:

Use the bigger brush to paint more.

Vary the tones from extreme dark to extreme light and grays as well.

UNIT 1: Experiment 3

Photocopy or print the image you used in the previous experiment.

Rule or draw a horizontal line across your selected pattern.

The pattern could be either horizontal or vertical (you choose).

The horizontal line represents the most distant part of your pattern.

Materials:

Very small amounts of black and white paint.

Two different sized brushes.

A pattern with a horizontal line.

Begin:

Use different combinations (black, gray, white) than previous experiment.

Paint over the pattern.

Try to add depth to the pattern using just tonal variations.

Initially draw with the brush and thin paint.

Then:

Make the foreground dark to a light background (like a fog).

Create harmonious areas by combining smaller tonal areas.

UNIT 1: Experiment 4

Photocopy or print out the image used in the previous experiment.

Rule or draw a horizontal line across your selected pattern.

The pattern could be either horizontal or vertical (you choose).

The horizontal line represents the most distant part of your pattern.

Materials:

Very small amounts of black and white paint.

Two different sized brushes.

A pattern with a horizontal line.

Begin:

Use different combinations (black, gray, white) than previous experiment.

Paint over the pattern.

Try to add depth to the pattern using just tonal variations.

Initially draw with the brush and thin paint.

Use the bigger brush to keep the shapes simple and broad (no details).

Then: Make the foreground dark to a light background (like a fog).

Space usually relates to emptiness or lack of precision like in distance.

UNIT 1: Experiment 5

Photocopy or print out the image used in the previous experiment.

Rule or draw a horizontal line across your selected pattern.

The pattern could be either horizontal or vertical (you choose).

The horizontal line represents the most distant part of your pattern.

Materials:

Very small amounts of black and white paint.

Two different sized brushes.

A pattern with a horizontal line.

Begin:

Use different combinations (black, gray, white) than previous experiment.

Paint over the pattern.

Try to add depth to the pattern using just tonal variations.

Initially draw with the brush and thin paint.

Use the bigger brush to keep the shapes simple and broad (no details).

Then: Make the foreground dark to a light background (like a fog).

Use thick or thin lines to show tonal variations.

UNIT 1: Experiment 6

Photocopy or print out the image used in the previous experiment.

Rule or draw a horizontal line across your selected pattern.

The pattern could be either horizontal or vertical (you choose).

The horizontal line represents the most distant part of your pattern.

Materials:

Very small amounts of black and white paint.

Two different sized brushes.

A pattern with a horizontal line.

Begin:

Use different combinations (black, gray, white) than previous experiment.

Paint over the pattern.

Try to add depth to the pattern using just tonal variations.

Initially draw with the brush and thin paint.

Use the bigger brush to keep the shapes simple and broad (no details).

Then:

Make the foreground dark to a light background (like a fog).

Show depth using tonal variations.

Further thoughts:

A picture or painting generally very light (HIGH KEY) the very darkest area will seem most advanced or nearest the viewer.

This applies even with abstract work as well.

Thus as depth recedes the tones become progressively lighter (like fog).

SECOND Experience Unit:

UNIT 2: Experiment 1
Photocopy or print out the image you have chosen.
You can modify size to conform to your Magic Multiple Miniatures.
Rule or draw a horizontal line across your selected pattern.
The pattern could be either horizontal or vertical (you choose).
The line could be ruled straight or drawn freely.
The line could even follow contours created by the shapes in your pattern.
The horizontal line represents the most distant part of your pattern.
Materials:
Use different materials from the previous unit (pencil, felt pen, chalk).
A pattern with a horizontal line.
Begin:
Shade in the pattern using strokes or long narrow marks. .
Try to add depth to the pattern using just tonal variation (dark and light).
Go from a light foreground to dark background (like night).

UNIT 2: Experiment 2
Photocopy or print out the image used in the previous experiment.
Rule or draw a horizontal line across your selected pattern.
The pattern could be either horizontal or vertical (you choose).
The horizontal line represents the most distant part of your pattern.
Materials:
Use the SAME materials as previous experiment (pencil, felt pen, chalk).
Also use the SAME pattern with a horizontal line.
Begin:
Shade in the pattern using strokes or long narrow marks. .
Try to add depth to the pattern using just tonal variation (dark and light).
Go from a light foreground to dark background (like night).
Keep the shapes simple and broad.

UNIT 2: Experiment 3

Photocopy or print out the image used in the previous experiment.

Rule or draw a horizontal line across your selected pattern.

The pattern could be either horizontal or vertical (you choose).

The horizontal line represents the most distant part of your pattern.
Materials:

Use the SAME materials as previous experiment (pencil, felt pen, chalk).

Also use the SAME pattern with a horizontal line.

Begin:

Shade in the pattern using strokes or long narrow marks. .

Try to add depth to the pattern using just tonal variation (dark and light).

Go from a light foreground to dark background (like night).

Keep the shapes simple and broad.

UNIT 2: Experiment 4

Photocopy or print out the image used in the previous experiment.

Rule or draw a horizontal line across your selected pattern.

The pattern could be either horizontal or vertical (you choose).

The horizontal line represents the most distant part of your pattern.
Materials:

Use the SAME materials as previous experiment (pencil, felt pen, chalk).

Also use the SAME pattern with a horizontal line.

Begin:

Shade in the pattern using strokes or long narrow marks. .

Then:

Add depth to the pattern using just tonal variation (dark and light).

Go from a light foreground to dark background (like night).

Keep the shapes simple and broad.

Use dissimilar tones (black and white) to show some contrast.

UNIT 2: Experiment 5

Photocopy or print out the image used in the previous experiment.

Rule or draw a horizontal line across your selected pattern.

The pattern could be either horizontal or vertical (you choose).

The horizontal line represents the most distant part of your pattern.

Materials:

Use the SAME materials as previous experiment (pencil, felt pen, chalk).

Also use the SAME pattern with a horizontal line.

Begin:

Shade in the pattern using strokes or long narrow marks.

These indicate a course or movement.

Then:

Add depth to the pattern using just tonal variation (dark and light).

Go from a light foreground to dark background (like night).

Show a plane or axis, may be horizontal, vertical or oblique as chosen.

UNIT 2: Experiment 6

Photocopy or print out the image used in the previous experiment.

Rule or draw a horizontal line across your selected pattern.

The pattern could be either horizontal or vertical (you choose).

The horizontal line represents the most distant part of your pattern.

Materials:

Use the SAME materials as previous experiment (pencil, felt pen, chalk).

Also use the SAME pattern with a horizontal line.

Begin:

Shade in the pattern using strokes or long narrow marks.

These indicate a course or movement.

Then:

Add depth to the pattern using just tonal variation (dark and light).

Go from a light foreground to dark background (like night).

Show a plane or axis, may be horizontal, vertical or oblique as chosen.

Further thoughts:
If a picture is generally dark (LOW KEY).
The lightest area will seem the most advanced or nearest the viewer.
This applies even with abstract work.
As depth recedes the tones become progressively darker (like night).

Major contrast is obvious (black and white).
Minor contrast is where there is little difference (dark grey and brown).

Direction link to a plane or axis, horizontal, vertical or oblique.
There is a start and end and can be seen in a serial order or sequence.
There is a link with rhythm and balance.

THIRD Experience Unit:

UNIT 3: Experiment 1
Photocopy or print out the image you have chosen.
Modify size to maintain conformity with your Magic Multiple Miniatures.
Rule or draw a horizontal line across your selected pattern.
The pattern could be either horizontal or vertical (you choose).
The line could be ruled straight or drawn freely.
The line could even follow contours created by the shapes in your pattern.
The horizontal line represents the most distant part of your pattern.
Materials:
Choose one of tonal materials from previous units. (pencil, felt pen, paint).
Begin:
Create large, small, and somewhere in between shapes.
Keep the shapes simple and broad.
Then:
Vary size of shapes to create light foreground to dark background (night).

UNIT 3: Experiment 2
Photocopy or print a DIFFERENT pattern than previous experiment.
Rule or draw a horizontal line across your selected pattern.
Modify size to maintain conformity with your Magic Multiple Miniatures.
The horizontal line represents the most distant part of your pattern.
Materials:
Use SAME materials as the previous experiment (pencil, felt pen, chalk).
Begin:
Repeat some tonal areas.
Use dark and light areas to show form.
Variety may be created by using contrast.
Then:
Use dark foreground to light background (like fog).
Develop repetition, gradation, alteration, radiation or sequence of marks.

UNIT 3: Experiment 3

Photocopy or print a DIFFERENT pattern than previous experiment.

Rule or draw a horizontal line across your selected pattern.

Modify size to maintain conformity with your Magic Multiple Miniatures.

The horizontal line represents the most distant part of your pattern.

Materials:

Use the SAME materials as previous experiment (pencil, felt pen, chalk).

Then:

Paint light foreground to dark background (like night).

Develop a repetition, gradation, alteration, radiation, sequence of marks.

UNIT 3: Experiment 4

Photocopy or print a DIFFERENT pattern than previous experiment.

Rule or draw a horizontal line across your selected pattern.

Modify size to maintain conformity with your Magic Multiple Miniatures.

The horizontal line represents the most distant part of your pattern.

Materials:

Use SAME materials as the previous experiment (pencil, felt pen, chalk).

Begin:

Create simple spheres, cones, cubes, pyramids, prisms, or ovoids.

Balance the shapes about an axis, or radiate them from a point.

Then:

Work from dark foreground to light background (like fog).

The factor indicates heavy or light weight, or density or solidity of matter.

UNIT 3: Experiment 5

Photocopy or print a DIFFERENT pattern than previous experiment.

Rule or draw a horizontal line across your selected pattern.

Modify size to maintain conformity with your Magic Multiple Miniatures.

The horizontal line represents the most distant part of your pattern.

Materials:

Use SAME materials as the previous experiment (pencil, felt pen, chalk).

Begin:

Dark foreground to light background (fog) OR light to dark (night).

Then:

Use soft (blurred) and hard (sharp) edges for modeling depth.

The boundary between different shapes is not always sharp or clear cut.

That means at times there should be a soft irregular transition.

UNIT 3: Experiment 6

Photocopy or print a DIFFERENT pattern than previous experiment.

Rule or draw a horizontal line across your selected pattern.

Modify size to maintain conformity with your Magic Multiple Miniatures.

The horizontal line represents the most distant part of your pattern.

Materials:

Use SAME materials as the previous experiment (pencil, felt pen, chalk).

Begin:

Dark foreground to light background (fog) OR light to dark (night).

Then:

Use contrast, radiation, majority area, or repetition of tone.

Emphasis of one aspect at the expense of another creates dominance.

Further thoughts:

ONE (fog/night) tonal depth technique consistently through the painting.

Some tonal parts may be dominant or subsidiary.

Exact repetition can lead to monotony.

Rhythm is related to direction.

The movement may be actual or implied.

Mass relates to space (occupation) is real (clay) or apparent (drawn).

DEVELOPMENT: Extensions
In the Development extension activities:
Draw on what you have learnt.

You can link what you have learned to your own goals.

DEVELOPMENT: Extension 1
Materials:
Use the SAME materials as used in a previous experiment from Unit One.

Use the SAME pattern as used in a previous experiment Unit One.
Begin:
BUT use only one of the tonal depth approaches.

Make sure it is consistent throughout the painting.

DEVELOPMENT: Extension 2
Materials:
Use the SAME materials as used in a previous experiment from Unit Two.

Use the SAME pattern as used in a previous experiment Unit Two.
Begin:
Add wholeness by an aspect dominant, or join aspects in a combination,

Make one aspect dominant by joining as combination or enclosing border.

Use only one of the tonal depth approaches.

DEVELOPMENT: Extension 3
Materials:
Use SAME materials as used in a previous experiment from Unit Three.

Use the SAME pattern as used in a previous experiment Unit Three.
Begin:
Use only one of the tonal depth approaches.

2. START: TEXTURAL DEPTH

FIRST Experience Unit:

UNIT 1: Experiment 1
Photocopy or print out the image you have chosen.
Modify size to maintain conformity with your Magic Multiple Miniatures.
Rule or draw a horizontal line across your selected pattern.
The pattern could be either horizontal or vertical (you choose).
The line could be ruled straight or drawn freely.
The line could even follow contours created by the shapes in your pattern.
The horizontal line represents the most distant part of your pattern.
Materials:
Very small amounts of black and white paint.
A brush.
A pattern with a horizontal line.
Begin:
Paint over the pattern.
Try to add depth to the pattern using just textural variations.

UNIT 1: Experiment 2

Photocopy or print the image you used in the previous experiment.

Rule or draw a horizontal line across your selected pattern.

The pattern could be either horizontal or vertical (you choose).

The horizontal line represents the most distant part of your pattern.

Materials:

Very small amounts of black and white paint.

Two different sized brushes.

A pattern with a horizontal line.

Begin:

Paint over the pattern.

Try to add depth to the pattern using just textural variations.

Initially draw with the brush and thin paint.

Then:

Use the bigger brush to paint more.

Vary the texture from very fine to coarser areas as well.

UNIT 1: Experiment 3

Photocopy or print the image you used in the previous experiment.

Rule or draw a horizontal line across your selected pattern.

The pattern could be either horizontal or vertical (you choose).

The horizontal line represents the most distant part of your pattern.

Materials:

Very small amounts of black and white paint.

Two different sized brushes.

A pattern with a horizontal line.

Begin:

Paint over the pattern.

Try to add depth to the pattern using just textural variations.

Initially draw with the brush and thin paint.

Then:

Make the foreground dark to a light background (like a fog).

Create harmonious areas by combining smaller textural areas.

UNIT 1: Experiment 4

Photocopy or print the image you used in the previous experiment.

Rule or draw a horizontal line across your selected pattern.

The pattern could be either horizontal or vertical (you choose).

The horizontal line represents the most distant part of your pattern.

Materials:

Very small amounts of black and white paint.

Two different sized brushes.

A pattern with a horizontal line.

Begin:

Paint over the pattern.

Try to add depth to the pattern using just textural variations.

Initially draw with the brush and thin paint.

Use the bigger brush to keep the shapes simple and broad (no details).

Then:

Make the foreground dark to a light background (like a fog).

Space relates to emptiness or lack of precision such as in distance.

UNIT 1: Experiment 5

Photocopy or print the image you used in the previous experiment.

Rule or draw a horizontal line across your selected pattern.

The pattern could be either horizontal or vertical (you choose).

The horizontal line represents the most distant part of your pattern.

Materials:

Very small amounts of black and white paint.

Two different sized brushes.

A pattern with a horizontal line.

Begin:

Paint over the pattern.

Try to add depth to the pattern using just textural variations.

Indicates a course of movement using texture.

This movement may be suggested.

Initially draw with the brush and thin paint.

Use the bigger brush to keep the shapes simple and broad (no details).

Then:

Make the foreground dark to a light background (like a fog).

Use thick or thin lines to show textural variations.

Direction relates to a plane or axis, may be horizontal, vertical or oblique.

UNIT 1: Experiment 6

Photocopy or print the image you used in the previous experiment.

Rule or draw a horizontal line across your selected pattern.

The pattern could be either horizontal or vertical (you choose).

The horizontal line represents the most distant part of your pattern.

Materials:

Very small amounts of black and white paint.

Two different sized brushes.

A pattern with a horizontal line.

Begin:

Paint over the pattern.

Try to add depth to the pattern using just textural variations.

Use texture to make some parts dominant or subsidiary.

Initially draw with the brush and thin paint.

Use the bigger brush to keep the shapes simple and broad (no details).

Then:

Make the foreground dark to a light background (like a fog).

Proportion is a comparison of parts.

Further thoughts:

A very light painting (HIGH KEY) the darkest area seems nearest viewer.

This applies even with abstract work.

As depth recedes textures are progressively lighter and fainter (like a fog).

SECOND Experience Unit:

UNIT 2: Experiment 1

Photocopy or print out the image you have chosen.

Modify the size to maintain conformity with Magic Multiple Miniatures.

Rule or draw a horizontal line across your selected pattern.

The pattern could be either horizontal or vertical (you choose).

The line could be ruled straight or drawn freely.

The line could even follow contours created by the shapes in your pattern.

The horizontal line represents the most distant part of your pattern.

Materials:

Use different materials from the previous unit (pencil, felt pen, chalk).

A pattern with a horizontal line.

Begin:

Shade in the pattern using strokes or long narrow marks. .

Add depth to the pattern using just textural variation (rough and smooth).

Then:

Go from a light foreground to dark background (like night).

Show a plane or axis, may be horizontal, vertical or oblique you choose.

UNIT 2: Experiment 2

Photocopy or print the image you used in the previous experiment.

Rule or draw a horizontal line across your selected pattern.

The pattern could be either horizontal or vertical (you choose).

The horizontal line represents the most distant part of your pattern.

Materials:

Use the SAME materials as previous experiment (pencil, felt pen, chalk).

Also use the SAME pattern with a horizontal line.

Begin: Shade in the pattern using strokes or long narrow marks. .

Add depth to the pattern using just textural variation (dark and light).

Then:

Go from a light foreground to dark background (like night).

Keep the shapes simple and broad.

Space may be open (incomplete) or closed (a boundary).

UNIT 2: Experiment 3

Photocopy or print the image you used in the previous experiment.

The pattern could be either horizontal or vertical (you choose).

The horizontal line represents the most distant part of your pattern.

Materials:

Use SAME materials as the previous experiment (pencil, felt pen, chalk).

Begin:

Fold the pattern down the centre.

Shade in the pattern using strokes or long narrow marks. .

Add depth to the pattern using just textural variation (dark and light).

Go from a light foreground to dark background (like night).

Then:

Go from a light foreground to dark background (like night).

Show a plane or axis, may be horizontal, vertical or oblique you choose.

Balance is equilibrium, stability or arrangement of parts in element.

UNIT 2: Experiment 4

Photocopy or print the image you used in the previous experiment.

Rule or draw a horizontal line across your selected pattern.

The pattern could be either horizontal or vertical (you choose).

The horizontal line represents the most distant part of your pattern.

Materials:

Use SAME materials as the previous experiment (pencil, felt pen, chalk).

Also use the SAME pattern with a horizontal line.

Begin:

Shade in the pattern using strokes or long narrow marks. .

Then:

Add depth to the pattern using just textural variation (dark and light).

Go from a light foreground to dark background (like night).

Keep the shapes simple and broad.

UNIT 2: Experiment 5
Photocopy or print the image you used in the previous experiment.
Rule or draw a horizontal line across your selected pattern.
The pattern could be either horizontal or vertical (you choose).
The horizontal line represents the most distant part of your pattern.
Materials:
Use SAME materials as the previous experiment (pencil, felt pen, chalk).
Begin:
Shade in the pattern using strokes or long narrow marks.
Create spheres, cones, cubes, pyramids, prisms, or ovoids.
These indicate a course or movement.
Then:
Add depth to the pattern using just textural variation (dark and light).
Go from a light foreground to dark background (like night).
Show a plane or axis, may be horizontal, vertical or oblique you choose.
Mass relates to space, may be real (lump of clay) or apparent (as drawn).

UNIT 2: Experiment 6
Photocopy or print the image you used in the previous experiment.
Rule or draw a horizontal line across your selected pattern.
The pattern could be either horizontal or vertical (you choose).
The horizontal line represents the most distant part of your pattern.
Materials:
Use SAME materials as the previous experiment (pencil, felt pen, chalk).
Also use the SAME pattern with a horizontal line.
Begin:
Shade in the pattern using strokes or long narrow marks.
These indicate a course or movement.
Enclose border to link smaller textured areas.
Then:
Add depth to the pattern using just textural variation (dark and light).
Go from a light foreground to dark background (like night).
Show a plane or axis, may be horizontal, vertical or oblique you choose.
Unity adds wholeness to a work.

Further thoughts:

A very light painting (HIGH KEY) the darkest area seems nearer a viewer.
This applies even with abstract work.

As depth recedes texture is progressively darker but less distinct (night).

Major contrast is obvious (rough and smooth).

Minor contrast is where little difference between the textural areas.

THIRD Experience Unit:
Use ONE template for a series of explorations of depth.

UNIT 3: Experiment 1
Photocopy or print out the image you have chosen.
Modify the size to maintain conformity with Magic Multiple Miniatures.
Rule or draw a horizontal line across your selected pattern.
The pattern could be either horizontal or vertical (you choose).
The line could be ruled straight or drawn freely.
The line could even follow contours created by the shapes in your pattern.
The horizontal line represents the most distant part of your pattern.
Materials:
Choose one of materials used in previous units. (pencil, felt pen, paint).
Begin:
Create large, small, or somewhere in between shapes.
Keep the shapes simple and broad.
Stress the textures at the expense of the shapes.
Then:
Vary sizes of shapes to create a light foreground to dark background (like night).
Stress on one aspect of an element at the expense of another creates dominance.

UNIT 3: Experiment 2

Photocopy or print a DIFFERENT pattern than previous experiment.

Rule or draw a horizontal line across your selected pattern.

Modify size to maintain conformity with your Magic Multiple Miniatures.

The horizontal line represents the most distant part of your pattern.

Materials:

Use SAME materials as the previous experiment (pencil, felt pen, chalk).

Begin:

Repeat some textural areas.

The shape sizes may be large, small, or somewhere in between.

Use dark and light areas to show form.

Variety may be created by using contrast.

Then:

Use dark foreground to light background (like fog).

Do a repetition, gradation, alteration, radiation or sequence of marks.

Size is the factor that indicates dimension.

UNIT 3: Experiment 3

Photocopy or print a DIFFERENT pattern than previous experiment.

Rule or draw a horizontal line across your selected pattern.

Modify size to maintain conformity with your Magic Multiple Miniatures.

The horizontal line represents the most distant part of your pattern.

Materials:

Use SAME materials as the previous experiment (pencil, felt pen, chalk).

Then:

Paint light foreground to dark background (like night).

Do a repetition, gradation, alteration, radiation or sequence of textures.

UNIT 3: Experiment 4
Photocopy or print a DIFFERENT pattern than previous experiment.
Rule or draw a horizontal line across your selected pattern.
Modify size to maintain conformity with your Magic Multiple Miniatures.
The horizontal line represents the most distant part of your pattern.
Materials:
Use SAME materials as the previous experiment (pencil, felt pen, chalk).
Begin:
Create simple spheres, cones, cubes, pyramids, prisms, or ovoids.
Balance the shapes about an axis, or radiate them from a point.
Then:
Work from dark foreground to light background (like fog).
The factor indicates heavy or light weight, or density or solidity of matter.

UNIT 3: Experiment 5
Photocopy or print a DIFFERENT pattern than previous experiment.
Rule or draw a horizontal line across your selected pattern.
Modify size to maintain conformity with your Magic Multiple Miniatures.
The horizontal line represents the most distant part of your pattern.
Materials:
Use SAME materials as the previous experiment (pencil, felt pen, chalk).
Begin:
Use a series of joined lines to define shapes, areas and spaces.
Dark foreground to light background (fog) OR light to dark (night).
Then:
Use soft (blurred) and hard (sharp) edges for modeling depth.
The boundary between different shapes is not always sharp or clear cut.
That means at times there should be a soft irregular transition.
Line has length and breadth where length is dominant.
Line is often two-dimensional (pencil) but is also three-dimensional (wire).

UNIT 3: Experiment 6

Photocopy or print a DIFFERENT pattern than previous experiment.

Rule or draw a horizontal line across your selected pattern.

Modify size to maintain conformity with your Magic Multiple Miniatures.

The horizontal line represents the most distant part of your pattern.

Materials:

Use SAME materials as the previous experiment (pencil, felt pen, chalk).

Begin:

Repeat or sequence many textural marks.

Dark foreground to light background (fog) OR light to dark (night).

Then:

Use contrast, radiation, majority area, or repetition of tone.

Emphasis of one aspect at the expense of another creates dominance.

Rhythm: movement, regular measured beat, flow, throb, pulse of element.

Further thoughts:

Use ONE (fog/night) tonal depth and be consistent through the painting.

Texture tends shows more clearly as it is closer.

Study this effect.

Some tonal parts may be dominant or subsidiary.

Exact repetition can lead to monotony.

Rhythm is related to direction.

The movement may be actual or implied.

Mass relates to space (occupation) is real (clay) or apparent (drawn).

DEVELOPMENT: Extensions
In the Development extension activities:
Draw on what you have learnt.

You can link what you have learned to your own goals.

DEVELOPMENT: Extension 1
Materials:
Use the SAME materials as used in a previous experiment from Unit One.

Use the SAME pattern as used in a previous experiment Unit One.
Begin:
BUT use only one of the textural depth approaches.

Make sure it is consistent throughout the experiment.

DEVELOPMENT: Extension 2
Materials:
Use the SAME materials as used in a previous experiment from Unit Two.

Use the SAME pattern as used in a previous experiment Unit Two.
Begin:
One aspect being dominant, or join aspects into a combination,

A dominant aspect (join as combination, enclose border) adds wholeness.

Use only one of the textural depth approaches.

DEVELOPMENT: Extension 3
Materials:
Use SAME materials as used in a previous experiment from Unit Three.

Use the SAME pattern as used in a previous experiment Unit Three.
Begin:
Use only one of the textural depth approaches.

Make sure it is consistent throughout the experiment.

3. START: COLOUR DEPTH

FIRST Experience Unit:
Use ONE template for a series of explorations of depth.

UNIT 1: Experiment 1
Photocopy or print out the image you have chosen.
Modify size to maintain conformity with your Magic Multiple Miniatures.
Rule or draw a horizontal line across your selected pattern.
The pattern could be either horizontal or vertical (you choose).
The line could be ruled straight or drawn freely.
The line could even follow contours created by the shapes in your pattern.
The horizontal line represents the most distant part of your pattern.
Materials:
Very small amounts of black and white paint and one colour.
A brush.
A pattern with a horizontal line.
Begin:
Paint over the pattern.
Try to add depth to the pattern using just colour variation (dark and light).

UNIT 1: Experiment 2
Photocopy or print the image you used in the previous experiment.
Rule or draw a horizontal line across your selected pattern.
The pattern could be either horizontal or vertical (you choose).
The horizontal line represents the most distant part of your pattern.
Materials:
Very small amounts of black and white paint and one colour.
Two different sized brushes.
A pattern with a horizontal line.
Begin:
Paint over the pattern.
Try to add depth to the pattern using just tonal variations.
Initially draw with the brush and thin paint.
Then:
Use the bigger brush to paint more.
Vary the colours from extreme dark to extreme light and grays as well.

UNIT 1: Experiment 3
Photocopy or print the image you used in the previous experiment.
Rule or draw a horizontal line across your selected pattern.
The pattern could be either horizontal or vertical (you choose).
The horizontal line represents the most distant part of your pattern.
Materials:
Very small amounts of black and white paint and one colour.
Two different sized brushes.
A pattern with a horizontal line.
Begin:
Paint over the pattern.
Try to add depth to the pattern using just tonal variations.
Initially draw with the brush and thin paint.
Then:
Make the foreground dark to a light background (like a fog).
Create harmonious areas by combining smaller coloured areas.

UNIT 1: Experiment 4
Photocopy or print the image you used in the previous experiment.
Rule or draw a horizontal line across your selected pattern.
The pattern could be either horizontal or vertical (you choose).
The horizontal line represents the most distant part of your pattern.
Materials:
Very small amounts of black and white paint and one colour.
Two different sized brushes.
A pattern with a horizontal line.
Begin:
Fold the pattern down the centre.
Paint over the pattern.
Try to add depth to the pattern using just colour variations.
Initially draw with the brush and thin paint.
Use the bigger brush to keep the shapes simple and broad (no details).
Then:
Make the foreground dark to a light background (like a fog).
Space usually relates to emptiness or lack of precision as in distance.
Balance may be symmetric (equal about an axis) like the folded pattern.

UNIT 1: Experiment 5

Photocopy or print the image you used in the previous experiment.

Rule or draw a horizontal line across your selected pattern.

The pattern could be either horizontal or vertical (you choose).

The horizontal line represents the most distant part of your pattern.

Materials:

Very small amounts of black and white paint and one colour.

Two different sized brushes.

A pattern with a horizontal line.

Begin:

Paint over the pattern.

Try to add depth to the pattern using just colour variations.

Make a start and an end to be seen in a serial order or sequence.

Initially draw with the brush and thin paint.

Use the bigger brush to keep the shapes simple and broad (no details).

Then:

Make the foreground dark to a light background (like a fog).

Use thick or thin lines to show colour variations.

Direction indicates an aim or course of movement.

UNIT 1: Experiment 6

Photocopy or print the image you used in the previous experiment.

Rule or draw a horizontal line across your selected pattern.

The pattern could be either horizontal or vertical (you choose).

The horizontal line represents the most distant part of your pattern.

Materials:

Very small amounts of black and white paint and one colour.

Two different sized brushes.

A pattern with a horizontal line.

Begin:

Paint over the pattern.

Try to add depth to the pattern using just colour variations.

Initially draw with the brush and thin paint.

Use the bigger brush to keep the shapes simple and broad (no details).

Then:

Make the foreground dark to a light background (like a fog).

Show depth using colour variations.

Further thoughts:

If a work is HIGH KEY the very darkest area seems nearest the viewer.

This applies even with abstract work.

As depth recedes the colours become progressively lighter (like a fog).

SECOND Experience Unit:

UNIT 2: Experiment 1
Photocopy or print out the image you have chosen.
Modify size to maintain conformity with your Magic Multiple Miniatures.
Rule or draw a horizontal line across your selected pattern.
The pattern could be either horizontal or vertical (you choose).
The line could be ruled straight or drawn freely.
The line could even follow contours created by the shapes in your pattern.
The horizontal line represents the most distant part of your pattern.
Materials:
Use different materials from the previous unit (pencil, felt pen, chalk).
A pattern with a horizontal line.
Begin:
Shade in the pattern using strokes or long narrow marks. .
Try to add depth to the pattern using just colour variation (dark and light).
Repeat many coloured marks.
Then:
Go from a light foreground to dark background (like night).
Rhythm is movement, regular measured beat, flow, throb, pulse of colour.

UNIT 2: Experiment 2

Photocopy or print the image you used in the previous experiment.

Rule or draw a horizontal line across your selected pattern.

The pattern could be either horizontal or vertical (you choose).

The horizontal line represents the most distant part of your pattern.

Materials:

Use SAME materials as the previous experiment (pencil, felt pen, chalk).

Also use the SAME pattern with a horizontal line.

Begin:

Shade in the pattern using strokes or long narrow marks. .

Leave some areas empty.

Try to add depth to the pattern using just colour variations.

Keep the shapes simple and broad.

Then:

Go from a light foreground to dark background (like night).

Space relates to lack of obvious elements (particularly mass and line).

UNIT 2: Experiment 3

Photocopy or print the image you used in the previous experiment.

Rule or draw a horizontal line across your selected pattern.

The pattern could be either horizontal or vertical (you choose).

The horizontal line represents the most distant part of your pattern.

Materials:

Use SAME materials as the previous experiment (pencil, felt pen, chalk).

Also use the SAME pattern with a horizontal line.

Begin:

Shade in the pattern using strokes or long narrow marks. .

Try to add depth to the pattern using just tonal variation (dark and light).

Go from a light foreground to dark background (like night).

Keep the shapes simple and broad.

UNIT 2: Experiment 4

Photocopy or print the image you used in the previous experiment.

Rule or draw a horizontal line across your selected pattern.

The pattern could be either horizontal or vertical (you choose).

The horizontal line represents the most distant part of your pattern.

Materials:

Use SAME materials as the previous experiment (pencil, felt pen, chalk).

Also use the SAME pattern with a horizontal line.

Begin:

Colour the pattern using strokes or long narrow marks. .

Show little difference between the colours used.

Then:

Add depth to the pattern using just tonal variation (dark and light).

Go from a light foreground to dark background (like night).

Keep the shapes simple and broad.

Use dissimilar tones (black and white) to show some contrast.

Minor contrast is where there is little difference (dark grey and brown).

Discord is extreme contrast (pale pink and orange).

UNIT 2: Experiment 5

Photocopy or print the image you used in the previous experiment.

The pattern could be either horizontal or vertical (you choose).

The horizontal line represents the most distant part of your pattern.

Materials:

Use SAME materials as the previous experiment (pencil, felt pen, chalk).

Also use the SAME pattern with a horizontal line.

Begin:

Colour the pattern using strokes or long narrow marks.

The marks indicate heavy or light weight, or density or solidity.

Then:

Add depth to the pattern using just tonal variation (dark and light).

Go from a light foreground to dark background (like night).

Mass relates to space may be real (lump of clay) or apparent (as drawn).

UNIT 2: Experiment 6

Photocopy or print the image you used in the previous experiment.

Rule or draw a horizontal line across your selected pattern.

The pattern could be either horizontal or vertical (you choose).

The horizontal line represents the most distant part of your pattern.

Materials:

Use SAME materials as the previous experiment (pencil, felt pen, chalk).

Also use the SAME pattern with a horizontal line.

Begin:

Colour the pattern using strokes or long narrow marks.

These indicate a course or movement.

Then:

Add depth to the pattern using just colour variations.

Go from a light foreground to dark background (like night).

Further thoughts:

If a picture is generally dark the very lightest area seems nearer a viewer.

This applies even with abstract work.

Thus as depth recedes tones become progressively darker (like at night).

Major contrast is obvious (black and white).

Minor contrast is where there is little difference (dark grey and brown).

Direction is horizontal, vertical or oblique about a plane or axis.

There is a start and an end and is seen in a serial order or sequence.

There is a link with rhythm and balance.

THIRD Experience Unit:

UNIT 3: Experiment 1
Photocopy or print out the image you have chosen.
Modify size to maintain conformity with your Magic Multiple Miniatures.
Rule or draw a horizontal line across your selected pattern.
The pattern could be either horizontal or vertical (you choose).
The line could be ruled straight or drawn freely.
The line could even follow contours created by the shapes in your pattern.
The horizontal line represents the most distant part of your pattern.
Materials:
Choose a coloured material used in past units. (pencil, felt pen, paint).
Begin:
Create large, small, and somewhere in between shapes.
Keep the shapes simple and broad.
Then:
Vary size of shapes for a light foreground to dark background (like night).

UNIT 3: Experiment 2
Photocopy or print a DIFFERENT pattern than previous experiment.
Rule or draw a horizontal line across your selected pattern.
Modify size to maintain conformity with your Magic Multiple Miniatures.
The horizontal line represents the most distant part of your pattern.
Materials:
Use SAME materials as the previous experiment (pencil, felt pen, chalk).
Begin:
Repeat some coloured areas.
They might share similar aspects (red orange and brown colours).
Variety may be created by using contrast.
Then:
Use dark foreground to light background (like fog).
The parts may be related through common use (biro and pencil).

UNIT 3: Experiment 3

Photocopy or print a DIFFERENT pattern than previous experiment.

Rule or draw a horizontal line across your selected pattern.

Modify size to maintain conformity with your Magic Multiple Miniatures.

The horizontal line represents the most distant part of your pattern.

Materials:

Use SAME materials as the previous experiment (pencil, felt pen, chalk).

Begin:

Use coloured strokes or long narrow marks.

They may be straight, curved, broken, jagged, flowing or a combination.

Then:

Paint light foreground to dark background (like night).

Line is the factor that indicates a row, series, course or contour.

A series of lines are joined, shape, area and space are defined by line.

UNIT 3: Experiment 4

Photocopy or print a DIFFERENT pattern than previous experiment.

Rule or draw a horizontal line across your selected pattern.

Modify size to maintain conformity with your Magic Multiple Miniatures.

The horizontal line represents the most distant part of your pattern.

Materials:

Use SAME materials as the previous experiment (pencil, felt pen, chalk).

Begin:

Vary the shapes so some parts are dominant and others subsidiary.

Then:

Work from dark foreground to light background (like fog).

Indicates heavy or light weight, or density or solidity of matter.

Proportion is a comparison of parts.

UNIT 3: Experiment 5
Photocopy or print a DIFFERENT pattern than previous experiment.
Rule or draw a horizontal line across your selected pattern.
Modify size to maintain conformity with your Magic Multiple Miniatures.
The horizontal line represents the most distant part of your pattern.
Materials:
Use SAME materials as the previous experiment (pencil, felt pen, chalk).
Begin:
Dark foreground to light background (fog) OR light to dark (night).
Then:
Use soft (blurred) and hard (sharp) edges for modeling depth.
The boundary between different shapes is not always sharp or clear cut.
That means at times there should be a soft irregular transition.

UNIT 3: Experiment 6
Photocopy or print a DIFFERENT pattern than previous experiment.
Rule or draw a horizontal line across your selected pattern.
Modify size to maintain conformity with your Magic Multiple Miniatures.
The horizontal line represents the most distant part of your pattern.
Materials:
Use SAME materials as the previous experiment (pencil, felt pen, chalk).
Begin:
Dark foreground to light background (fog) OR light to dark (night).
Then:
Use contrast, radiation, majority area, or repetition of tone.
Emphasis of one aspect at the expense of another creates dominance.

Further thoughts:
Use ONE (fog/night) tonal depth technique per painting consistently.
Some tonal parts may be dominant or subsidiary.
Exact repetition can lead to monotony.
Rhythm is related to direction.
The movement may be actual or implied.
Mass relates to space and may be real (lump clay) or apparent (drawn).

DEVELOPMENT: Extensions
In the Development extension activities:
Draw on what you have learnt.

You can link what you have learned to your own goals.

DEVELOPMENT: Extension 1
Materials:
Use the SAME materials as used in a previous experiment from Unit One.

Use the SAME pattern as used in a previous experiment Unit One.
Begin:
BUT use only one of the colour depth approaches.

Make sure it is consistent throughout the painting.

DEVELOPMENT: Extension 2
Materials:
Use the SAME materials as used in a previous experiment from Unit Two.

Use the SAME pattern as used in a previous experiment Unit Two.
Begin:
Add wholeness by an aspect dominant, or join aspects in a combination,

Make an aspect dominant by joining as combination or using a border.

Use only one of the colour depth approaches.

DEVELOPMENT: Extension 3
Materials:
Use the SAME materials as in a previous experiment from Unit Three.

Use the SAME pattern as used in a previous experiment Unit Three.
Begin:
Use only one of the colour depth approaches.

4. START: SHAPE DEPTH

FIRST Experience Unit:
Use ONE template for a series of explorations of depth.
Decide which template you will work with.

UNIT 1: Experiment 1
Photocopy or print out the image you have chosen.
Modify size to maintain conformity with your Magic Multiple Miniatures.
Rule or draw a horizontal line across your selected pattern.
The pattern could be either horizontal or vertical (you choose).
The line could be ruled straight or drawn freely.
The line could even follow contours created by the shapes in your pattern.
The horizontal line represents the most distant part of your pattern.
Materials:
Very small amounts of black and white paint and a colour.
A brush.
A pattern with a horizontal line.
Begin:
Paint over the pattern.
Try to add depth to the pattern using just shape variations.
Then:
Use the bigger brush to paint more.

UNIT 1: Experiment 2

Photocopy or print the image you used in the previous experiment.

Rule or draw a horizontal line across your selected pattern.

The pattern could be either horizontal or vertical (you choose).

The horizontal line represents the most distant part of your pattern.

Materials:

Very small amounts of black and white paint and a colour.

Two different sized brushes.

A pattern with a horizontal line.

Begin:

Paint over the pattern.

Add depth to the pattern using just shape variations.

Then:

Use the bigger brush to paint more.

UNIT 1: Experiment 3

Photocopy or print the image you used in the previous experiment.

Rule or draw a horizontal line across your selected pattern.

The pattern could be either horizontal or vertical (you choose).

The horizontal line represents the most distant part of your pattern.

Materials:

Very small amounts of black and white paint and a colour.

Two different sized brushes.

A pattern with a horizontal line.

Begin:

Paint over the pattern.

Try to add depth to the pattern using just shape variations.

Has a start and an end and can be seen in a serial order or sequence.

Initially draw with the brush and thin paint.

Then:

Make the foreground dark to a light background (like a fog).

Create harmonious areas by combining smaller tonal areas.

Direction indicates aim or course of movement.

The movement may be actual or suggested.

UNIT 1: Experiment 4

Photocopy or print the image you used in the previous experiment.

Rule or draw a horizontal line across your selected pattern.

The pattern could be either horizontal or vertical (you choose).

The horizontal line represents the most distant part of your pattern.

Materials:

Very small amounts of black and white paint and a colour.

Two different sized brushes.

A pattern with a horizontal line.

Begin:

Paint over the pattern.

Try to add depth to the pattern using just shape variations.

They might share similar aspects (all round).

Initially draw with the brush and thin paint.

Use the bigger brush to keep the shapes simple and broad (no details).

Then: Make the foreground dark to a light background (like a fog).

Unity concerns agreement, closeness, relatedness or similarity of parts.

UNIT 1: Experiment 5

Photocopy or print the image you used in the previous experiment.

Rule or draw a horizontal line across your selected pattern.

The pattern could be either horizontal or vertical (you choose).

The horizontal line represents the most distant part of your pattern.

Materials:

Very small amounts of black and white paint and a colour.

Two different sized brushes.

A pattern with a horizontal line.

Begin:

Paint over the pattern.

Try to add depth to the pattern using just shape variations.

Initially draw with the brush and thin paint.

Use the bigger brush to keep the shapes simple and broad (no details).

Then: Make the foreground dark to a light background (like a fog).

Use thick or thin lines to show tonal variations.

UNIT 1: Experiment 6

Photocopy or print the image you used in the previous experiment.

Rule or draw a horizontal line across your selected pattern.

The pattern could be either horizontal or vertical (you choose).

The horizontal line represents the most distant part of your pattern.

Materials:

Very small amounts of black and white paint and a colour.

Two different sized brushes.

A pattern with a horizontal line.

Begin:

Paint over the pattern.

Try to add depth to the pattern using just shape variations.

Consider actual or implied areas between shapes.

Initially draw with the brush and thin paint.

Use the bigger brush to keep the shapes simple and broad (no details).

Then:

Make the foreground dark to a light background (like a fog).

Show depth using shape variations.

Space relates to the lack of obvious elements (particularly mass and line).

Further thoughts:

A very light painting has the darkest area will seem nearest a viewer.

This applies even with abstract work.

As depth recedes the tones become progressively lighter (like a fog).

SECOND Experience Unit:

UNIT 2: Experiment 1
Photocopy or print out the image you have chosen.
Modify size to maintain conformity with your Magic Multiple Miniatures.
Rule or draw a horizontal line across your selected pattern.
The pattern could be either horizontal or vertical (you choose).
The line could be ruled straight or drawn freely.
The line could even follow contours created by the shapes in your pattern.
The horizontal line represents the most distant part of your pattern.
Materials:
Use different materials from the previous unit (pencil, felt pen, chalk).
A pattern with a horizontal line.
Begin:
Shade in the pattern using strokes or long narrow marks. .
Try to add depth to the pattern using just shape variations.
Go from a light foreground to dark background (like night).
Some parts may be dominant or subsidiary.
Then: Make the foreground dark to a light background (like a fog).
Show depth using shape variations.
Proportion is a comparison of parts.

UNIT 2: Experiment 2
Photocopy or print the image you used in the previous experiment.
Rule or draw a horizontal line across your selected pattern.
The pattern could be either horizontal or vertical (you choose).
The horizontal line represents the most distant part of your pattern.
Materials:
Use SAME materials as the previous experiment (pencil, felt pen, chalk).
Also use the SAME pattern with a horizontal line.
Begin:
Shade in the pattern using strokes or long narrow marks. .
Try to add depth to the pattern using just tonal variation (dark and light).
Then: Go from a light foreground to dark background (like night).
Keep the shapes simple and broad.

UNIT 2: Experiment 3

Photocopy or print the image you used in the previous experiment.

The pattern could be either horizontal or vertical (you choose).

The horizontal line represents the most distant part of your pattern.

Materials:

Use SAME materials as the previous experiment (pencil, felt pen, chalk).

Also use the SAME pattern with a horizontal line.

Begin:

Shade in the pattern using strokes or long narrow marks. .

Try to add depth to the pattern using just shape variations.

Go from a light foreground to dark background (like night).

The shapes may be large, small, or somewhere in between.

Then:

Go from a light foreground to dark background (like night).

Keep the shapes simple and broad.

Size indicates dimension.

UNIT 2: Experiment 4

Photocopy or print the image you used in the previous experiment.

Rule or draw a horizontal line across your selected pattern.

The pattern could be either horizontal or vertical (you choose).

The horizontal line represents the most distant part of your pattern.

Materials:

Use SAME materials as the previous experiment (pencil, felt pen, chalk).

Begin:

Shade in the pattern using strokes or long narrow marks. .

They may be straight, curved, broken, jagged, flowing or some combination of these.

Then:

Add depth to the pattern using just shape variations.

Go from a light foreground to dark background (like night).

Keep the shapes simple and broad.

A series of lines joined, shape, area and space are defined by the line.

UNIT 2: Experiment 5

Photocopy or print the image you used in the previous experiment.

Rule or draw a horizontal line across your selected pattern.

The horizontal line represents the most distant part of your pattern.

Materials:

Use SAME materials as the previous experiment (pencil, felt pen, chalk).

Also use the SAME pattern with a horizontal line.

Begin:

Shade in the pattern using strokes or long narrow marks.

Show an equilibrium, stability or arrangement of parts within the pattern.

Then:

Add depth to the pattern using just shape variations.

Go from a light foreground to dark background (like night).

Balance: symmetric (about axis), radiate (from point) or asymmetric.

UNIT 2: Experiment 6

Photocopy or print the image you used in the previous experiment.

Rule or draw a horizontal line across your selected pattern.

The pattern could be either horizontal or vertical (you choose).

The horizontal line represents the most distant part of your pattern.

Materials:

Use SAME materials as the previous experiment (pencil, felt pen, chalk).

Also use the SAME pattern with a horizontal line.

Begin:

Shade in the pattern using strokes or long narrow marks.

These indicate a course or movement.

Cohesion, integration, standardization or singleness of parts in shapes.

Then:

Add depth to the pattern using just tonal variation (dark and light).

Go from a light foreground to dark background (like night).

Show a plane or axis, may be horizontal, vertical or oblique you choose.

Unity adds wholeness to a work.

Further thoughts:
If a picture is generally dark the lightest area will seem most advanced.
This applies even with abstract work.
Thus as depth recedes tones become progressively darker (like at night).

Major contrast is obvious (black and white).
Minor contrast is where there is little difference (dark grey and brown).

Direction relates to a plane or axis is horizontal, vertical or oblique.
There is a start and end and can be seen in a serial order or sequence.
There is a link with rhythm and balance.

THIRD Experience Unit:

UNIT 3: Experiment 1
Photocopy or print out the image you have chosen.
Modify size to maintain conformity with your Magic Multiple Miniatures.
Rule or draw a horizontal line across your selected pattern.
The pattern could be either horizontal or vertical (you choose).
The line could be ruled straight or drawn freely.
The line could even follow contours created by the shapes in your pattern.
The horizontal line represents the most distant part of your pattern.
Materials:
Choose a tonal material used in previous units. (pencil, felt pen, paint).
Begin:
Create large, small, and somewhere in between shapes.
Keep the shapes simple and broad.
But stress the important parts.
Then:
Vary sizes of shapes for a light foreground to dark background (like night).
Emphasis may be by using contrast, radiation, majority area, or repetition.

UNIT 3: Experiment 2
Photocopy or print a DIFFERENT pattern than previous experiment.
Rule or draw a horizontal line across your selected pattern.
Modify size to maintain conformity with your Magic Multiple Miniatures.
The horizontal line represents the most distant part of your pattern.
Materials:
Use the SAME materials as previous experiment (pencil, felt pen, chalk).
Begin:
Repeat some shapes.
Use dark and light areas to show form.
Variety may be created by using contrast.
Then:
Use dark foreground to light background (like fog).

UNIT 3: Experiment 3

Photocopy or print a DIFFERENT pattern than previous experiment.

Rule or draw a horizontal line across your selected pattern.

Modify size to maintain conformity with your Magic Multiple Miniatures.

The horizontal line represents the most distant part of your pattern.

Materials:

Use SAME materials as the previous experiment (pencil, felt pen, chalk).

Begin:

Create simple spheres, cones, cubes, pyramids, prisms, or ovoids.

Balance the shapes about an axis, or radiate them from a point.

Modify shapes to indicate heavy or light weight.

Then:

Paint light foreground to dark background (like night).

Develop repetition, gradation, alteration, radiation or sequence of marks.

Mass relates to space and may be real (lump clay) or apparent (drawn).

UNIT 3: Experiment 4

Photocopy or print a DIFFERENT pattern than previous experiment.

Rule or draw a horizontal line across your selected pattern.

Modify size to maintain conformity with your Magic Multiple Miniatures.

The horizontal line represents the most distant part of your pattern.

Materials:

Use SAME materials as the previous experiment (pencil, felt pen, chalk).

Begin:

Change shapes in the pattern to create greater contrast.

Variety may be created by using shape contrast.

Then:

Work from dark foreground to light background (like fog).

Major contrast is obvious.

Minor contrast is where there is little difference.

UNIT 3: Experiment 5
Photocopy or print a DIFFERENT pattern than previous experiment.
Rule or draw a horizontal line across your selected pattern.
Modify size to maintain conformity with your Magic Multiple Miniatures.
The horizontal line represents the most distant part of your pattern.
Materials:
Use SAME materials as the previous experiment (pencil, felt pen, chalk).
Begin:
Use soft (blurred) and hard (sharp) edges for modeling depth.
The boundary between different shapes is not always sharp or clear cut.
That means at times there should be a soft irregular transition.
Then:
Dark foreground to light background (fog) OR light to dark (night).

UNIT 3: Experiment 6
Photocopy or print a DIFFERENT pattern than previous experiment.
Rule or draw a horizontal line across your selected pattern.
Modify size to maintain conformity with your Magic Multiple Miniatures.
The horizontal line represents the most distant part of your pattern.
Materials:
Use SAME materials as the previous experiment (pencil, felt pen, chalk).
Begin:
Create shapes that have a regular measured beat.
Then:
Dark foreground to light background (fog) OR light to dark (night).
Rhythm is repetition, gradation, alteration, radiation, sequence of marks.
Rhythm is related to direction.

Further thoughts:
Use ONE (fog/night) tonal depth technique per painting consistently.
Some tonal parts may be dominant or subsidiary.
Exact repetition can lead to monotony.
Rhythm is related to direction.
The movement may be actual or implied.
Mass links to space (occupy) and may be real (clay) or apparent (drawn).

DEVELOPMENT: Extensions
In the Development extension activities:
Draw on what you have learnt.

You can link what you have learned to your own goals.

DEVELOPMENT: Extension 1
Materials:
Use the SAME materials as used in a previous experiment from Unit One.

Use the SAME pattern as used in a previous experiment Unit One.
Begin:
BUT use only one of the shape depth approaches.

Make sure it is consistent throughout the painting.

DEVELOPMENT: Extension 2
Materials:
Use the SAME materials as used in a previous experiment from Unit Two.

Use the SAME pattern as used in a previous experiment Unit Two.
Begin:
Add wholeness by an aspect dominant, or join aspects in a combination,

Make one aspect dominant by joining combination or enclosing a border.

Use only one of the shape depth approaches.

DEVELOPMENT: Extension 3
Materials:
Use SAME materials as used in a previous experiment from Unit Three.

Use the SAME pattern as used in a previous experiment Unit Three.
Begin:
Use only one of the shape depth approaches.

3. LIGHT:

START: TONAL LIGHT

UNIT 1: Experiment 1
Photocopy or print out the image you have chosen.
Modify the size to maintain conformity with your Magic Multiple Miniatures.
Rule or draw a vertical line through your selected pattern.
The pattern could be either horizontal or vertical (you choose).
The line could be ruled straight or drawn freely.
The line could even follow contours created by the shapes in your pattern.
The vertical line represents the closest part of your pattern.
Materials:
Very small amounts of black and white paint.
A brush.
A pattern with a vertical line.
Begin:
Paint over the pattern.
Try to add light to the pattern using just tonal variation (dark and light).

UNIT 1: Experiment 2
Photocopy or print out the image you used in the previous experiment.
Rule or draw a vertical line across your selected pattern.
The pattern could be either horizontal or vertical (you choose).
The vertical line represents the closest part of your pattern.
Materials:
Very small amounts of black and white paint.
Two different sized brushes.
A pattern with a vertical line.
Begin:
Paint over the pattern.
Try to add light to the pattern using just tonal variations.
Keep the tones similar.
Initially draw with the brush and thin paint.
Then:
Use the bigger brush to paint more.
Vary the tones from extreme dark to extreme light and grays as well.
Tonal harmony concerns agreement, closeness, relatedness or similarity.

UNIT 1: Experiment 3
Photocopy or print out the image you used in the previous experiment.
Rule or draw a vertical line across your selected pattern.
The pattern could be either horizontal or vertical (you choose).
The vertical line represents the closest part of your pattern.
Materials:
Very small amounts of black and white paint.
Two different sized brushes.
A pattern with a vertical line.
Begin:
Paint over the pattern.
Try to add light to the pattern using just tonal variations.
Initially draw with the brush and thin paint.
Then:
Make the foreground dark to a light background (like a fog).
Create harmonious areas by combining smaller tonal areas.

UNIT 1: Experiment 4

Photocopy or print out the image you used in the previous experiment.

Rule or draw a vertical line across your selected pattern.

The pattern could be either horizontal or vertical (you choose).

The vertical line represents the closest part of your pattern.

Materials:

Very small amounts of black and white paint.

Two different sized brushes.

A pattern with a vertical line.

Begin:

Paint over the pattern.

Try to add light to the pattern using just tonal variations.

Emphasize dissimilar tonal areas (black and white).

Initially draw with the brush and thin paint.

Use the bigger brush to keep the shapes simple and broad (no details).

Then: Make the foreground dark to a light background (like a fog).

Space usually relates to emptiness or lack of precision such as in distance.

Variety may be created by using contrast.

UNIT 1: Experiment 5

Photocopy or print out the image you used in the previous experiment.

Rule or draw a vertical line across your selected pattern.

The pattern could be either horizontal or vertical (you choose).

The vertical line represents the closest part of your pattern.

Materials:

Very small amounts of black and white paint.

Two different sized brushes.

A pattern with a vertical line.

Begin:

Paint over the pattern.

Try to add light to the pattern using just tonal variations.

Initially draw with the brush and thin paint.

Use the bigger brush to keep the shapes simple and broad (no details).

Then: Make the foreground dark to a light background (like a fog).

Use thick or thin lines to show tonal variations.

UNIT 1: Experiment 6

Photocopy or print out the image you used in the previous experiment.

Rule or draw a vertical line across your selected pattern.

The pattern could be either horizontal or vertical (you choose).

The vertical line represents the closest part of your pattern.

Materials:

Very small amounts of black and white paint.

Two different sized brushes.

A pattern with a vertical line.

Begin:

Paint over the pattern.

Try to add light to the pattern using just tonal variations.

Use strokes or long narrow marks.

May be straight, curved, broken, jagged, flowing or a combination of these.

Initially draw with the brush and thin paint.

Use the bigger brush to keep the shapes simple and broad (no details).

Then:

Make the foreground dark to a light background (like a fog).

Show light using tonal variations.

Line is the factor that indicates a row, series, course or contour.

When a series of lines are joined, shape, area and space are defined by line.

Line is two-dimensional (pencil lines) but can be three-dimensional (wire).

Further thoughts:

If a picture or painting is generally very light (HIGH KEY) the very darkest area will seem to be the most advanced or nearest the viewer.

This applies even with abstract work.

Thus as light recedes the tones become progressively lighter (like a fog).

SECOND Experience Unit:

UNIT 2: Experiment 1
Photocopy or print out the image you have chosen.
Rule or draw a vertical line across your selected pattern.
The pattern could be either horizontal or vertical (you choose).
The line could be ruled straight or drawn freely.
The line could even follow contours created by the shapes in your pattern.
The vertical line represents the closest part of your pattern.
Materials:
Use different materials from the previous unit (pencil, felt pen, chalk).
A pattern with a vertical line.
Begin:
Shade in the pattern using strokes or long narrow marks. .
Try to add light to the pattern using just tonal variation (dark and light).
Go from a light foreground to dark background (like night).
Then:
Add light to the pattern using just tonal variation (dark and light).
Go from a light foreground to dark background (like night).
Keep the shapes simple and broad.
Use dissimilar tones (black and white) to show some contrast.

UNIT 2: Experiment 2

Photocopy or print out the image you used in the previous experiment.

The pattern could be either horizontal or vertical (you choose).

The vertical line represents the closest part of your pattern.

Materials:

Use the SAME materials as the previous experiment (pencil, felt pen, chalk).

Also use the SAME pattern with a vertical line.

Begin:

Shade in the pattern using strokes or long narrow marks. .

Try to add light to the pattern using just tonal variation (dark and light).

Make marks using repetition, gradation, alteration, radiation or sequence.

Then: Add light to the pattern using just tonal variation (dark and light).

Go from a light foreground to dark background (like night).

Keep the shapes simple and broad.

Use dissimilar tones (black and white) to show some contrast.

Rhythm: movement, regular measured beat, flow, throb, pulsation in element.

UNIT 2: Experiment 3

Photocopy or print out the image you used in the previous experiment.

Rule or draw a vertical line across your selected pattern.

The pattern could be either horizontal or vertical (you choose).

The vertical line represents the closest part of your pattern.

Materials:

Use the SAME materials as the previous experiment (pencil, felt pen, chalk).

Also use the SAME pattern with a vertical line.

Begin:

Shade in the pattern using strokes or long narrow marks. .

Try to add light to the pattern using just tonal variation (dark and light).

Go from a light foreground to dark background (like night).

Keep the shapes simple and broad.

Then:

Add light to the pattern using just tonal variation (dark and light).

Go from a light foreground to dark background (like night).

Keep the shapes simple and broad.

Use dissimilar tones (black and white) to show some contrast.

UNIT 2: Experiment 4

Photocopy or print out the image you used in the previous experiment.

Rule or draw a vertical line across your selected pattern.

The pattern could be either horizontal or vertical (you choose).

The vertical line represents the closest part of your pattern.

Materials:

Use the SAME materials as the previous experiment (pencil, felt pen, chalk).

Also use the SAME pattern with a vertical line.

Begin:

Shade in the pattern using strokes or long narrow marks. .

The shape sizes created may be large, small, or somewhere in between.

Then:

Add light to the pattern using just tonal variation (dark and light).

Go from a light foreground to dark background (like night).

Keep the shapes simple and broad.

Use dissimilar tones (black and white) to show some contrast.

Size is the factor that indicates dimension.

UNIT 2: Experiment 5

Photocopy or print out the image you used in the previous experiment.

Rule or draw a vertical line across your selected pattern.

The pattern could be either horizontal or vertical (you choose).

The vertical line represents the closest part of your pattern.

Materials:

Use the SAME materials as the previous experiment (pencil, felt pen, chalk).

Also use the SAME pattern with a vertical line.

Begin:

Shade in the pattern using strokes or long narrow marks.

These indicate a course or movement.

Make some parts dominant and others subsidiary.

Then:

Add light to the pattern using just tonal variation (dark and light).

Go from a light foreground to dark background (like night).

Proportion is a comparison of parts.

UNIT 2: Experiment 6

Photocopy or print out the image you used in the previous experiment.

Rule or draw a vertical line across your selected pattern.

The pattern could be either horizontal or vertical (you choose).

The vertical line represents the closest part of your pattern.

Materials:

Use the SAME materials as the previous experiment (pencil, felt pen, chalk).

Also use the SAME pattern with a vertical line.

Begin:

Shade in the pattern using strokes or long narrow marks.

These indicate heavy or light weight.

Then:

Add light to the pattern using just tonal variation (dark and light).

Go from a light foreground to dark background (like night).

Show a plane or axis, may be horizontal, vertical or oblique as you choose.

Mass occupies space and may be real (lump of clay) or apparent (as drawn).

Further thoughts:

If a picture is generally dark (LOW KEY) the very lightest area will seem to be the most advanced or nearest the viewer.

This applies even with abstract work.

Thus as light recedes the tones become progressively darker (like at night).

Major contrast is obvious (black and white).

Minor contrast is where there is little difference (dark grey and brown).

Direction links to a plane or axis, may be horizontal, vertical or oblique.

There is a start and an end and can be seen in a serial order or sequence.

There is a link with rhythm and balance.

THIRD Experience Unit:

UNIT 3: Experiment 1
Photocopy or print out the image you have chosen.
Modify the size to maintain conformity with your Magic Multiple Miniatures.
Rule or draw a vertical line across your selected pattern.
The pattern could be either horizontal or vertical (you choose).
The line could be ruled straight or drawn freely.
The line could even follow contours created by the shapes in your pattern.
The vertical line represents the closest part of your pattern.
Materials:
Choose one tonal material used in the previous units. (pencil, felt pen, paint).
Begin:
Create large, small, of somewhere in between shapes.
Keep the shapes simple and broad.
Use contrast, radiation, majority area, or repetition.
Then: Vary sizes of shapes for a light foreground dark background (night).
Emphasis of an aspect of an element over another creates dominance.

UNIT 3: Experiment 2
Photocopy or print a DIFFERENT pattern than for the previous experiment.
Rule or draw a vertical line across your selected pattern.
Modify the size to maintain conformity with your Magic Multiple Miniatures.
The vertical line represents the closest part of your pattern.
Materials:
Use the SAME materials as the previous experiment (pencil, felt pen, chalk).
Begin:
Repeat some tonal areas.
Use dark and light areas to show form.
Variety may be created by using contrast.
Show equilibrium, stability or an arrangement of tonal areas.
Then: Use dark foreground to light background (like fog).
Develop a repetition, gradation, alteration, radiation or sequence of marks.
Balance is symmetric (about an axis), radiate (from a point) or asymmetric.

UNIT 3: Experiment 3

Photocopy or print a DIFFERENT pattern than the previous experiment.

Rule or draw a vertical line across your selected pattern.

Modify the size to maintain conformity with your Magic Multiple Miniatures.

The vertical line represents the closest part of your pattern.

Materials:

Use the SAME materials as the previous experiment (pencil, felt pen, chalk).

Begin:

Create simple spheres, cones, cubes, pyramids, prisms, or ovoids.

Balance the shapes about an axis, or radiate them from a point.

Then:

Paint light foreground to dark background (like night).

Develop a repetition, gradation, alteration, radiation or sequence of marks.

UNIT 3: Experiment 4

Photocopy or print a DIFFERENT pattern than the previous experiment.

Rule or draw a vertical line across your selected pattern.

Modify the size to maintain conformity with your Magic Multiple Miniatures.

The vertical line represents the closest part of your pattern.

Materials:

Use the SAME materials as the previous experiment (pencil, felt pen, chalk).

Begin:

Create simple spheres, cones, cubes, pyramids, prisms, or ovoids.

Balance the shapes about an axis, or radiate them from a point.

Use tones to show being inside, outside, under or over.

Then:

Work from dark foreground to light background (like fog).

The factor that indicates heavy or light weight, or density or solidity of matter.

Space relates to a lack of obvious other element (particularly mass and line).

UNIT 3: Experiment 5

Photocopy or print a DIFFERENT pattern than the previous experiment.

Rule or draw a vertical line across your selected pattern.

Modify the size to maintain conformity with your Magic Multiple Miniatures.

The vertical line represents the closest part of your pattern.

Materials:

Use the SAME materials as the previous experiment (pencil, felt pen, chalk).

Begin:

Use soft (blurred) and hard (sharp) edges for modeling light.

The boundary between different shapes is not always sharp or clear cut.

That means at times there should be a soft irregular transition.

Make one tone dominant by enclosing a border.

Then:

Dark foreground to light background (fog) OR light to dark (night).

Unity adds wholeness to a work.

UNIT 3: Experiment 6

Photocopy or print a DIFFERENT pattern than the previous experiment.

Rule or draw a vertical line across your selected pattern.

Modify the size to maintain conformity with your Magic Multiple Miniatures.

The vertical line represents the closest part of your pattern.

Materials:

Use the SAME materials as the previous experiment (pencil, felt pen, chalk).

Begin:

Use contrast, radiation, majority area, or repetition of tone.

Emphasis of tone at the expense of colour creates tonal dominance.

Create a start and an end that can be seen in a sequence.

Then:

Dark foreground to light background (fog) OR light to dark (night).

Direction is the factor that indicates aim or course of movement.

The movement may be actual or suggested.

Further thoughts:

Use only ONE (fog/night) tonal light technique in any painting.

Then be consistent throughout the painting.

Some tonal parts may be dominant or subsidiary.

Exact repetition can lead to monotony.

Rhythm is related to direction.

The movement may be actual or implied.

Mass relates to space and may be real (lump of clay) or apparent (as drawn).

DEVELOPMENT: Extensions

In the Development extension activities:

Draw on what you have learnt.

You can link what you have learned to your own goals.

DEVELOPMENT: Extension 1

Materials:

Use the SAME materials as used in a previous experiment from Unit One.

Use the SAME pattern as used in a previous experiment Unit One.

Begin:

BUT use only one of the tonal light approaches.

Make sure it is consistent throughout the painting.

DEVELOPMENT: Extension 2

Materials:

Use the SAME materials as used in a previous experiment from Unit Two.

Use the SAME pattern as used in a previous experiment Unit Two.

Begin:

Add wholeness by one aspect dominant, or join aspects into a combination,

Make an aspect dominant by joining as a combination or enclosing a border.

Use only one of the tonal light approaches.

DEVELOPMENT: Extension 3

Materials:

Use the SAME materials as used in a previous experiment from Unit Three.

Use the SAME pattern as used in a previous experiment Unit Three.

Begin: Use only one of the tonal light approaches.

START: TEXTURE LIGHT

UNIT 1: Experiment 1
Photocopy or print out the image you have chosen.
Modify the size to maintain conformity with your Magic Multiple Miniatures.
Rule or draw a vertical line through your selected pattern.
The pattern could be either horizontal or vertical (you choose).
The line could be ruled straight or drawn freely.
The line could even follow contours created by the shapes in your pattern.
The vertical line represents the closest part of your pattern.
Materials:
Very small amounts of black and white paint.
A brush.
A pattern with a vertical line.
Begin: Paint over the pattern.
Try to add light to the pattern using just tonal variation (dark and light).

UNIT 1: Experiment 2
Photocopy or print out the image you used in the previous experiment.
Rule or draw a vertical line across your selected pattern.
The pattern could be either horizontal or vertical (you choose).
The vertical line represents the closest part of your pattern.
Materials:
Very small amounts of black and white paint.
Two different sized brushes.
A pattern with a horizontal line.
Begin: Paint over the pattern.
Try to add light to the pattern using just tonal variations.
Initially draw with the brush and thin paint.
Show an impression of movement.
Then use the bigger brush to paint more.
Vary the tones from extreme dark to extreme light and grays as well.
Direction links to a plane or axis, which may be horizontal, vertical or oblique.

UNIT 1: Experiment 3

Photocopy or print out the image you used in the previous experiment.

Rule or draw a vertical line across your selected pattern.

The vertical line represents the closest part of your pattern.

Materials:

Very small amounts of black and white paint.

Two different sized brushes.

A pattern with a vertical line.

Begin:

Paint over the pattern and add light using just tonal variations.

Initially draw with the brush and thin paint.

Then:

Make the foreground dark to a light background (like a fog).

Create harmonious areas by combining smaller tonal areas.

UNIT 1: Experiment 4

Photocopy or print out the image you used in the previous experiment.

The pattern could be either horizontal or vertical (you choose).

The vertical line represents the closest part of your pattern.

Materials:

Very small amounts of black and white paint.

Two different sized brushes.

A pattern with a vertical line.

Begin:

Paint adding light to the pattern using just tonal variations.

Initially draw with the brush and thin paint.

Use the bigger brush to keep the shapes simple and broad (no details).

There should be a relatedness or similarity of textures.

Then:

Make the foreground dark to a light background (like a fog).

Harmony usually relates to similar aspects in a pattern.

UNIT 1: Experiment 5

Photocopy or print out the image you used in the previous experiment.

The pattern could be either horizontal or vertical (you choose).

The vertical line represents the closest part of your pattern.

Materials:

Very small amounts of black and white paint.

Two different sized brushes.

A pattern with a vertical line.

Begin:

Paint over the pattern and add light using just tonal variations.

Initially draw with the brush and thin paint.

Use the bigger brush to keep the shapes simple and broad (no details).

Then:

Make the foreground dark to a light background (like a fog).

Use thick or thin lines to show tonal variations.

UNIT 1: Experiment 6

Photocopy or print out the image you used in the previous experiment.

Rule or draw a vertical line across your selected pattern.

The pattern could be either horizontal or vertical (you choose).

The vertical line represents the closest part of your pattern.

Materials:

Very small amounts of black and white paint.

Two different sized brushes.

A pattern with a vertical line.

Begin:

Paint over the pattern.

Try to add light to the pattern using just tonal variations.

Initially draw with the brush and thin paint.

Use the bigger brush to keep the shapes simple and broad (no details).

Add texture using strokes or long narrow marks.

Then:

Make the foreground dark to a light background (like a fog).

Show light using textural variations.

Line is straight, curved, broken, jagged, flowing or a combination of these.

Further activities:

If a picture or painting is generally very light (HIGH KEY) the very darkest area will seem to be the most advanced or nearest the viewer.

This applies even with abstract work.

Thus as light recedes the tones become progressively lighter (like a fog).

SECOND Experience Unit:

UNIT 2: Experiment 1
Photocopy or print out the image you have chosen.
Modify the size to maintain conformity with your Magic Multiple Miniatures.
Rule or draw a vertical line across your selected pattern.
The pattern could be either horizontal or vertical (you choose).
The line could be ruled straight or drawn freely.
The line could even follow contours created by the shapes in your pattern.
The vertical line represents the closest part of your pattern.
Materials:
Use different materials from the previous unit (pencil, felt pen, chalk).
A pattern with a vertical line.
Begin:
Shade in the pattern using strokes or long narrow marks. .
Try to add light to the pattern using just tonal variation (dark and light).
Then:
Make the foreground dark to a light background (like a fog).
Show light using textural variations.

UNIT 2: Experiment 2

Photocopy or print out the image you used in the previous experiment.

Rule or draw a vertical line across your selected pattern.

The pattern could be either horizontal or vertical (you choose).

The vertical line represents the closest part of your pattern.

Materials:

Use the SAME materials as the previous experiment (pencil, felt pen, chalk).

Also use the SAME pattern with a vertical line.

Begin:

Shade in the pattern using strokes or long narrow marks. .

Try to add light to the pattern using just tonal variation (dark and light).

Go from a light foreground to dark background (like night).

Keep the shapes simple and broad.

Make some textures dominant and other subsidiary.

Then:

Make the foreground dark to a light background (like a fog).

Show light using textural variations.

Proportion is a comparison of parts.

UNIT 2: Experiment 3

Photocopy or print out the image you used in the previous experiment.

The pattern could be either horizontal or vertical (you choose).

The vertical line represents the closest part of your pattern.

Materials:

Use the SAME materials as the previous experiment (pencil, felt pen, chalk).

Also use the SAME pattern with a vertical line.

Begin:

Shade in the pattern using strokes or long narrow marks. .

Try to add light to the pattern using just textural variation.

Then:

Go from a light foreground to dark background (like night).

Keep the shapes simple and broad.

Use dissimilar tones (black and white) to show some contrast.

UNIT 2: Experiment 4

Photocopy or print out the image you used in the previous experiment.

Rule or draw a vertical line across your selected pattern.

The pattern could be either horizontal or vertical (you choose).

The vertical line represents the closest part of your pattern.

Materials:

Use the SAME materials as the previous experiment (pencil, felt pen, chalk).

Also use the SAME pattern with a vertical line.

Begin:

Shade in the pattern using strokes or long narrow marks. .

Make different textures some large, others small, or somewhere in between.

Then:

Try to add light to the pattern using just textural variation.

Go from a light foreground to dark background (like night).

Use dissimilar tones (black and white) to show some contrast.

Size is the factor that indicates dimension.

UNIT 2: Experiment 5

Photocopy or print out the image you used in the previous experiment.

Rule or draw a vertical line across your selected pattern.

The pattern could be either horizontal or vertical (you choose).

The vertical line represents the closest part of your pattern.

Materials:

Use the SAME materials as the previous experiment (pencil, felt pen, chalk).

Also use the SAME pattern with a vertical line.

Begin:

Shade in the pattern using strokes or long narrow marks.

Use dissimilar textures.

Then:

Try to add light to the pattern using just textural variation.

Go from a light foreground to dark background (like night).

Variety may be created by using contrast.

UNIT 2: Experiment 6

Photocopy or print out the image you used in the previous experiment.

Rule or draw a vertical line across your selected pattern.

The pattern could be either horizontal or vertical (you choose).

The vertical line represents the closest part of your pattern.

Materials:

Use the SAME materials as the previous experiment (pencil, felt pen, chalk).

Also use the SAME pattern with a vertical line.

Begin:

Shade in the pattern using strokes or long narrow marks.

These indicate a course or movement.

Use textural contrast to focus on a majority area.

Then:

Add light to the pattern using just tonal variation (dark and light).

Go from a light foreground to dark background (like night).

Show a plane or axis, may be horizontal, vertical or oblique as you choose.

Emphasis of one aspect of an element at the expense of another creates dominance.

Further thoughts:

If generally dark (LOW KEY) the very lightest area seems nearest the viewer.

This applies even with abstract work.

Thus as light recedes the tones become progressively darker (like at night).

Major contrast is obvious (black and white).

Minor contrast is where there is little difference (dark grey and brown).

Direction relates to a plane or axis, horizontal, vertical or oblique.

There is a start and an end and can be seen in a serial order or sequence.

There is a link with rhythm and balance.

THIRD Experience Unit:

UNIT 3: Experiment 1
Photocopy or print out the image you have chosen.
Modify the size to maintain conformity with your Magic Multiple Miniatures.
Rule or draw a vertical line across your selected pattern.
The pattern could be either horizontal or vertical (you choose).
The line could be ruled straight or drawn freely.
The line could even follow contours created by the shapes in your pattern.
The vertical line represents the closest part of your pattern.
Materials:
Choose one tonal material used in the previous units. (pencil, felt pen, paint).
Begin:
Create large, small, of somewhere in between shapes.
Keep the shapes simple and broad.
Then:
Vary sizes of shapes to create a light foreground to dark background (night).

UNIT 3: Experiment 2
Photocopy or print a DIFFERENT pattern than the previous experiment.
Rule or draw a vertical line across your selected pattern.
Modify the size to maintain conformity with your Magic Multiple Miniatures.
The vertical line represents the closest part of your pattern.
Materials:
Use the SAME materials as the previous experiment (pencil, felt pen, chalk).
Begin:
Repeat some tonal areas.
Use dark and light areas to show form.
Variety may be created by using contrast.
Add cohesion, integration, standardization or singleness of textures.
Then:
Use dark foreground to light background (like fog).
Develop a repetition, gradation, alteration, radiation or sequence of marks.
Unity adds wholeness to a work.

UNIT 3: Experiment 3
Photocopy or print a DIFFERENT pattern than the previous experiment.
Rule or draw a vertical line across your selected pattern.
Modify the size to maintain conformity with your Magic Multiple Miniatures.
The vertical line represents the closest part of your pattern.
Materials:
Use the SAME materials as the previous experiment (pencil, felt pen, chalk).
Begin:
Fold the pattern in the centre.
Repeat some textural areas either side of the fold.
Then:
Paint light foreground to dark background (like night).
Develop a repetition, gradation, alteration, radiation or sequence of marks.
Balance is equilibrium, stability or arrangement of parts in an element.

UNIT 3: Experiment 4
Photocopy or print a DIFFERENT pattern than the previous experiment.
Rule or draw a vertical line across your selected pattern.
Modify the size to maintain conformity with your Magic Multiple Miniatures.
The vertical line represents the closest part of your pattern.
Materials:
Use the SAME materials as the previous experiment (pencil, felt pen, chalk).
Begin:
Create simple spheres, cones, cubes, pyramids, prisms, or ovoids.
Balance the shapes about an axis, or radiate them from a point.
Leave areas empty.
Then:
Work from dark foreground to light background (like fog).
The factor that indicates heavy or light weight, or density or solidity of matter.
Space links the lack of obvious other element (particularly mass and line).

UNIT 3: Experiment 5

Photocopy or print a DIFFERENT pattern than the previous experiment.

Rule or draw a vertical line across your selected pattern.

Modify the size to maintain conformity with your Magic Multiple Miniatures.

The vertical line represents the closest part of your pattern.

Materials:

Use the SAME materials as the previous experiment (pencil, felt pen, chalk).

Begin:

Use soft (blurred) and hard (sharp) edges for modeling light.

The boundary between different shapes is not always sharp or clear cut.

That means at times there should be a soft irregular transition.

Repeat textures in sequences.

Then:

Dark foreground to light background (fog) OR light to dark (night).

Rhythm is related to direction.

UNIT 3: Experiment 6

Photocopy or print a DIFFERENT pattern than the previous experiment.

Rule or draw a vertical line across your selected pattern.

Modify the size to maintain conformity with your Magic Multiple Miniatures.

The vertical line represents the closest part of your pattern.

Materials:

Use the SAME materials as the previous experiment (pencil, felt pen, chalk).

Begin:

Use contrast, radiation, majority area, or repetition of tone.

Emphasis of one aspect at the expense of another creates dominance.

Use texture to show heavy or light weight.

Then:

Dark foreground to light background (fog) OR light to dark (night).

Mass relates to space and may be real (lump of clay) or apparent (as drawn).

Further thoughts:

Use only ONE (fog/night) tonal light technique in any painting.

Then be consistent throughout the painting.

Some tonal parts may be dominant or subsidiary.

Exact repetition can lead to monotony.

Rhythm is related to direction.

The movement may be actual or implied.

Mass links to space (occupation) and may be real (clay) or apparent (drawn).

DEVELOPMENT: Extensions
In the Development extension activities:
Draw on what you have learnt.

You can link what you have learned to your own goals.

DEVELOPMENT: Extension 1
Materials:
Use the SAME materials as used in a previous experiment from Unit One.

Use the SAME pattern as used in a previous experiment Unit One.
Begin:
BUT use only one of the textural light approaches.

Make sure it is consistent throughout the painting.

DEVELOPMENT: Extension 2
Materials:
Use the SAME materials as used in a previous experiment from Unit Two.

Use the SAME pattern as used in a previous experiment Unit Two.
Begin:
Add wholeness to a work by dominant texture,

Make one aspect dominant by joining as a combination or enclose a border.

Use only one of the textural light approaches.

DEVELOPMENT: Extension 3
Materials:
Use the SAME materials as used in a previous experiment from Unit Three.

Use the SAME pattern as used in a previous experiment Unit Three.
Begin:
Use only one of the textural light approaches.

START: COLOUR LIGHT

FIRST Experience Unit:
UNIT 1: Experiment 1
Photocopy or print out the image you have chosen.
Modify the size to maintain conformity with your Magic Multiple Miniatures.
Rule or draw a vertical line through your selected pattern.
The pattern could be either horizontal or vertical (you choose).
The line could be ruled straight or drawn freely.
The line could even follow contours created by the shapes in your pattern.
The vertical line represents the closest part of your pattern.
Materials:
Very small amounts of black and white paint and one colour.
A brush.
A pattern with a vertical line.
Begin:
Paint over the pattern.
Try to add light to the pattern using just colour variations.

UNIT 1: Experiment 2
Photocopy or print out the image you used in the previous experiment.
Rule or draw a vertical line across your selected pattern.
The pattern could be either horizontal or vertical (you choose).
The vertical line represents the closest part of your pattern.
Materials:
Very small amounts of black and white paint and one colour.
Two different sized brushes.
A pattern with a vertical line.
Begin:
Paint over the pattern.
Try to add light to the pattern using just tonal variations.
Initially draw with the brush and thin paint.
Then:
Use the bigger brush to paint more.
Vary the colours from extreme dark to extreme light.

UNIT 1: Experiment 3
Photocopy or print out the image you used in the previous experiment.
Rule or draw a vertical line across your selected pattern.
The pattern could be either horizontal or vertical (you choose).
The vertical line represents the closest part of your pattern.
Materials:
Very small amounts of black and white paint and one colour.
Two different sized brushes.
A pattern with a vertical line.
Begin:
Paint over the pattern.
Try to add light to the pattern using just colour variations.
Initially draw with the brush and thin paint.
Then:
Make the foreground dark to a light background (like a fog).
Create harmonious areas by combining smaller coloured areas.

UNIT 1: Experiment 4
Photocopy or print out the image you used in the previous experiment.
Rule or draw a vertical line across your selected pattern.
The pattern could be either horizontal or vertical (you choose).
The vertical line represents the closest part of your pattern.
Materials:
Very small amounts of black and white paint and one colour.
Two different sized brushes.
A pattern with a horizontal line.
Begin:
Paint over the pattern.
Try to add light to the pattern using just colour variations.
Use colour to show density or solidity of areas.
Initially draw with the brush and thin paint.
Use the bigger brush to keep the shapes simple and broad (no details).
Then make the foreground dark to a light background (like a fog).
Space usually relates to emptiness or lack of precision such as in distance.
Mass relates to space and may be real (lump of clay) or apparent (as drawn).

UNIT 1: Experiment 5

Photocopy or print out the image you used in the previous experiment.

Rule or draw a vertical line across your selected pattern.

The pattern could be either horizontal or vertical (you choose).

The vertical line represents the closest part of your pattern.

Materials:

Very small amounts of black and white paint and one colour.

Two different sized brushes.

A pattern with a vertical line.

Begin:

Paint over the pattern.

Try to add light to the pattern using just colour variations.

They might share similar aspects such as red orange and brown colours.

Initially draw with the brush and thin paint.

Use the bigger brush to keep the shapes simple and broad (no details).

Then make the foreground dark to a light background (like a fog).

Use thick or thin lines to show tonal variations.

Harmony concerns agreement, closeness, relatedness or similarity of parts.

UNIT 1: Experiment 6

Photocopy or print out the image you used in the previous experiment.

Rule or draw a vertical line across your selected pattern.

The pattern could be either horizontal or vertical (you choose).

The vertical line represents the closest part of your pattern.

Materials:

Very small amounts of black and white paint and two colours.

Two different sized brushes.

A pattern with a vertical line.

Begin:

Paint over the pattern.

Try to add light to the pattern using just colour variations.

Initially draw with the brush and thin paint.

Use the bigger brush to keep the shapes simple and broad (no details).

Then make the foreground dark to a light background (like a fog).

Show light using colour variations.

Further thoughts:

If a picture or painting is generally very light (HIGH KEY).

The very darkest area seems the most advanced or nearest the viewer.

This applies even with abstract work.

Thus as light recedes the colours become progressively lighter (like a fog).

SECOND Experience Unit:

UNIT 2: Experiment 1
Photocopy or print out the image you have chosen.
Rule or draw a vertical line across your selected pattern.
The pattern could be either horizontal or vertical (you choose).
The line could be ruled straight or drawn freely.
The line could even follow contours created by the shapes in your pattern.
The vertical line represents the closest part of your pattern.
Materials:
Use different materials from the previous unit (pencil, felt pen, chalk).
A pattern with a vertical line.
Begin:
Shade in the pattern using coloured strokes or long narrow marks. .
Try to add light to the pattern using just colour variations.
Use some dissimilar colours.
Discord is extreme contrast (pale pink and orange).
Then:
Go from a light foreground to dark background (like night).
Rhythm is movement, regular measured beat, flow, throb, pulsation of colour.
Major contrast is obvious (black and white).
Minor contrast is where there is little difference (dark grey and brown).

UNIT 2: Experiment 3
Photocopy or print out the image you used in the previous experiment.
The pattern could be either horizontal or vertical (you choose).
The vertical line represents the closest part of your pattern.
Materials:
Use the SAME materials as the previous experiment (pencil, felt pen, chalk).
Also use the SAME pattern with a vertical line.
Begin:
Shade in the pattern using strokes or long narrow marks. .
Try to add light to the pattern using just colour variations.
Keep the shapes simple and broad.
Use colour to stress on important parts.
Then:
Go from a light foreground to dark background (like night).
Space links to the lack of obvious other element (particularly mass and line).
Emphasis of one area of an element at the expense of another is dominance.

UNIT 2: Experiment 4
Photocopy or print out the image you used in the previous experiment.
Rule or draw a vertical line across your selected pattern.
The pattern could be either horizontal or vertical (you choose).
The vertical line represents the closest part of your pattern.
Materials:
Use the SAME materials as the previous experiment (pencil, felt pen, chalk).
Also use the SAME pattern with a vertical line.
Begin:
Shade in the pattern using coloured strokes or long narrow marks. .
Leave areas to indicate emptiness.
Then:
Add light to the pattern using just tonal variation (dark and light).
Go from a light foreground to dark background (like night).
Use dissimilar tones (black and white) to show some contrast.
Space relates to lack of obvious other element (particularly mass and line).

UNIT 2: Experiment 5
Photocopy or print out the image you used in the previous experiment.
Rule or draw a vertical line across your selected pattern.
The pattern could be either horizontal or vertical (you choose).
The vertical line represents the closest part of your pattern.
Materials:
Use the SAME materials as the previous experiment (pencil, felt pen, chalk).
Also use the SAME pattern with a vertical line.
Begin:
Colour the pattern using strokes or long narrow marks.
These indicate a course or movement.
Make one aspect dominant by enclosing a border.
Then:
Add light to the pattern using just tonal variation (dark and light).
Go from a light foreground to dark background (like night).
A plane or axis, which may be horizontal, vertical or oblique as you choose.
Unity adds wholeness to a work.

UNIT 2: Experiment 6
Photocopy or print out the image you used in the previous experiment.
Rule or draw a horizontal line across your selected pattern.
The pattern could be either horizontal or vertical (you choose).
The vertical line represents the closest part of your pattern.
Materials:
Use the SAME materials as the previous experiment (pencil, felt pen, chalk).
Also use the SAME pattern with a vertical line.
Begin:
Colour the pattern using strokes or long narrow marks.
These indicate a course or movement.
The strokes may be large, small, or somewhere in between.
Then:
Add light to the pattern using just colour variations (warm to cool).
Go from a light foreground to dark background (like night).
A plane or axis, which may be vertical, vertical or oblique as you choose.
Size is the factor that indicates dimension.

Further thoughts:

A picture generally dark the very lightest area will seem to be the most advanced.

This applies even with abstract work.

Thus as light recedes the tones become progressively darker (like at night).

Major contrast is obvious (warm and cool).

Minor contrast is where there is little difference (dark grey and brown).

Direction links to plane or axis, and is horizontal, vertical or oblique.

There is a start and an end and can be seen in a serial order or sequence.

There is a link with rhythm and balance.

THIRD Experience Unit:

UNIT 3: Experiment 1
Photocopy or print out the image you have chosen.
Modify the size to maintain conformity with your Magic Multiple Miniatures.
Rule or draw a vertical line across your selected pattern.
The pattern could be either horizontal or vertical (you choose).
The line could be ruled straight or drawn freely.
The line could even follow contours created by the shapes in your pattern.
The vertical line represents the closest part of your pattern.
Materials:
Choose one colour material used in previous units. (pencil, felt pen, paint).
Begin:
Create large, small, of somewhere in between shapes.
Keep the shapes simple and broad.
Create colour areas that are dominant or subsidiary.
Then:
Vary sizes of shapes for a light foreground to dark background (like night).
Proportion is a comparison of parts.

UNIT 3: Experiment 2
Photocopy or print a DIFFERENT pattern than the previous experiment.
Rule or draw a vertical line across your selected pattern.
Modify the size to maintain conformity with your Magic Multiple Miniatures.
The vertical line represents the closest part of your pattern.
Materials:
Use the SAME materials as the previous experiment (pencil, felt pen, chalk).
Begin:
Repeat some colour areas.
Use dark and light areas to show form.
Variety may be created by using colour contrast.
Then:
Use dark foreground to light background (like fog).
Develop a repetition, gradation, alteration, radiation or sequence of marks.

UNIT 3: Experiment 3

Photocopy or print a DIFFERENT pattern than the previous experiment.

Modify the size to maintain conformity with your Magic Multiple Miniatures.

The vertical line represents the closest part of your pattern.

Materials:

Use the SAME materials as the previous experiment (pencil, felt pen, chalk).

Begin:

Repeat some colour areas.

Use warm and cool areas to show form.

Variety may be created by using contrast.

Also show an equilibrium, stability or arrangement of coloured areas

Then:

Paint light foreground to dark background (like night).

Develop a repetition, gradation, alteration, radiation or sequence of marks.

Balance may be actual or implied.

UNIT 3: Experiment 4

Photocopy or print a DIFFERENT pattern than the previous experiment.

Rule or draw a vertical line across your selected pattern.

Modify the size to maintain conformity with your Magic Multiple Miniatures.

The vertical line represents the closest part of your pattern.

Materials:

Use the SAME materials as the previous experiment (pencil, felt pen, chalk).

Begin:

Create simple spheres, cones, cubes, pyramids, prisms, or ovoids.

Use colour to show a course of movement through the pattern.

There is a start and an end.

Then:

Work from dark foreground to light background (like fog).

The factor that indicates heavy or light weight, or density or solidity of matter.

Direction link to a plane or axis, which may be horizontal, vertical or oblique.

There is a link with rhythm and balance.

UNIT 3: Experiment 5

Photocopy or print a DIFFERENT pattern than the previous experiment.

Rule or draw a vertical line across your selected pattern.

Modify the size to maintain conformity with your Magic Multiple Miniatures.

The vertical line represents the closest part of your pattern.

Materials:

Use the SAME materials as the previous experiment (pencil, felt pen, chalk).

Begin:

Use soft (blurred) and hard (sharp) edges for modeling light.

At times there should be a soft irregular colour transition.

The movement may be actual or implied.

Then:

Dark foreground to light background (fog) OR light to dark (night).

Rhythm is related to direction.

UNIT 3: Experiment 6

Photocopy or print a DIFFERENT pattern than the previous experiment.

Rule or draw a vertical line across your selected pattern.

Modify the size to maintain conformity with your Magic Multiple Miniatures.

The vertical line represents the closest part of your pattern.

Materials:

Use the SAME materials as the previous experiment (pencil, felt pen, chalk).

Begin:

Use contrast, radiation, majority area, or repetition of colour.

Emphasis of one aspect of colour at the expense of another.

When a series of lines are joined, shape, area and space may be defined.

Then:

Dark foreground to light background (fog) OR light to dark (night).

Line is straight, curved, broken, jagged, flowing or a combination of these.

Line often two-dimensional (flat pencil lines) but can be 3 dimensional (wire).

Further thoughts:
Use only ONE (fog/night) tonal light technique in any painting.
Then be consistent throughout the painting.
Some tonal parts may be dominant or subsidiary.
Exact repetition can lead to monotony.
Rhythm is related to direction.
The movement may be actual or implied.
Mass relates to space and may be real (lump of clay) or apparent (as drawn).

DEVELOPMENT: Extensions
Draw on what you have learnt.
You can link what you have learned to your own goals.

DEVELOPMENT: Extension 1
Materials:
Use the SAME materials as used in a previous experiment from Unit One.
Use the SAME pattern as used in a previous experiment Unit One.
Begin:
BUT use only one of the colour light approaches.
Make sure it is consistent throughout the painting.

DEVELOPMENT: Extension 2
Materials:
Use the SAME materials as used in a previous experiment from Unit Two.
Use the SAME pattern as used in a previous experiment Unit Two.
Begin:
Add wholeness by an aspect dominant, or join aspects into a combination,
Make an aspect dominant by joining as a combination or enclosing a border.
Use only one of the colour light approaches.

DEVELOPMENT: Extension 3
Materials:
Use the SAME materials as used in a previous experiment from Unit Three.
Use the SAME pattern as used in a previous experiment Unit Three.
Begin:
Use only one of the colour light approaches.

START: SHAPE LIGHT

FIRST Experience Unit:

UNIT 1: Experiment 1
Photocopy or print out the image you have chosen.
The pattern could be either horizontal or vertical (you choose).
Rule or draw a vertical line through your selected pattern.
Line is ruled straight, drawn freely or follow contours from the pattern shapes.
The vertical line represents the closest part of your pattern.
Materials:
Very small amounts of black and white paint and two colours.
A brush.
A pattern with a vertical line.
Begin:
Paint over the pattern.
Try to add light to the pattern using just linear variation (thin and thick).
These may be strokes or long narrow marks.
Then:
Use the bigger brush to paint more.
A series of lines are joined, shape, area and space are defined by line.

UNIT 1: Experiment 2

Photocopy or print out the image you used in the previous experiment.

The pattern could be either horizontal or vertical (you choose).

The vertical line represents the closest part of your pattern.

Materials:

Very small amounts of black and white paint and two colours.

Two different sized brushes.

A pattern with a horizontal line.

Begin:

Paint over the pattern initially draw with the brush and thin paint.

Add light to the pattern using just shape variations.

Some parts may be dominant or subsidiary.

Then:

Use the bigger brush to paint more.

Vary the tones from extreme dark to extreme light and grays as well.

Proportion is a comparison of parts.

UNIT 1: Experiment 3

Photocopy or print out the image you used in the previous experiment.

Rule or draw a vertical line across your selected pattern.

The pattern could be either horizontal or vertical (you choose).

The vertical line represents the closest part of your pattern.

Materials:

Very small amounts of black and white paint and two colours.

Two different sized brushes.

A pattern with a vertical line.

Begin:

Paint over the pattern initially draw with the brush and thin paint.

Add light to the pattern using just shape variations.

Imply a balance of shapes.

Then:

Make the foreground dark to a light background (like a fog).

Create harmonious areas by combining smaller tonal areas.

Balance is symmetric (equal on axis), radiate (from a point) or asymmetric.

UNIT 1: Experiment 4

Photocopy or print out the image you used in the previous experiment.

Rule or draw a vertical line across your selected pattern.

The pattern could be either horizontal or vertical (you choose).

The vertical line represents the closest part of your pattern.

Materials:

Very small amounts of black and white paint and two colours.

Two different sized brushes.

A pattern with a vertical line.

Begin:

Paint over the pattern.

Try to add light to the pattern using just shape variations.

Initially draw with the brush and thin paint.

Use the bigger brush to keep the shapes simple and broad (no details).

Unity adds wholeness to a work.

Then make the foreground dark to a light background (like a fog).

Space usually relates to emptiness or lack of precision such as in distance.

Unity adds wholeness to a work.

UNIT 1: Experiment 5

Photocopy or print out the image you used in the previous experiment.

Rule or draw a vertical line across your selected pattern.

The pattern could be either horizontal or vertical (you choose).

The vertical line represents the closest part of your pattern.

Materials:

Very small amounts of black and white paint and two colours.

Two different sized brushes.

A pattern with a vertical line.

Begin:

Paint over pattern add light to the pattern using just size variations of shapes.

Initially draw with the brush and thin paint.

Use the bigger brush to keep the shapes simple and broad (no details).

Then make the foreground dark to a light background (like a fog).

Use thick or thin lines to show tonal variations.

Size may be large, small, of somewhere in between.

UNIT 1: Experiment 6

Photocopy or print out the image you used in the previous experiment.

Rule or draw a vertical line across your selected pattern.

The pattern could be either horizontal or vertical (you choose).

The vertical line represents the closest part of your pattern.

Materials:

Very small amounts of black and white paint and two colours.

Two different sized brushes.

A pattern with a vertical line.

Begin:

Paint over the pattern.

Try to add light to the pattern using just shape variations.

Initially draw with the brush and thin paint.

Use the bigger brush to keep the shapes simple and broad (no details).

Use contrasting shapes.

Then:

Make the foreground dark to a light background (like a fog).

Show light using tonal variations.

Emphasis of one aspect of an element at the expense of another creates dominance.

Further thoughts:

A picture or painting is very light (HIGH KEY).

The darkest area will seem to be the most advanced or nearest the viewer.

This applies even with abstract work.

Thus as light recedes the tones become progressively lighter (like a fog).

SECOND Experience Unit:

UNIT 2: Experiment 1
Photocopy or print out the image you have chosen.
Modify the size to maintain conformity with your Magic Multiple Miniatures.
Rule or draw a vertical line across your selected pattern.
The pattern could be either horizontal or vertical (you choose).
The line could be ruled straight or drawn freely.
The line could even follow contours created by the shapes in your pattern.
The vertical line represents the closest part of your pattern.
Materials:
Use different materials from the previous unit (pencil, felt pen, chalk).
A pattern with a vertical line.
Begin:
Shade in the pattern using strokes or long narrow marks. .
Try to add light to the pattern using just shape variation (big and small).
Then:
Make the foreground dark to a light background (like a fog).
Show light using shape variations.
Proportion is a comparison of parts.

UNIT 2: Experiment 2

Photocopy or print out the image you used in the previous experiment.

Rule or draw a vertical line across your selected pattern.

The pattern could be either horizontal or vertical (you choose).

The vertical line represents the closest part of your pattern.

Materials:

Use the SAME materials as the previous experiment (pencil, felt pen, chalk).

Also use the SAME pattern with a vertical line.

Begin:

Shade in the pattern using strokes or long narrow marks. .

Show light using shape variations.

Keep the shapes simple and broad.

Use the shapes to show heavy or light weight.

Then:

Go from a light foreground to dark background (like night).

Proportion is a comparison of parts.

Simple forms of mass are sphere, cone, cube, pyramid, prism, or ovoid.

UNIT 2: Experiment 3

Photocopy or print out the image you used in the previous experiment.

The pattern could be either horizontal or vertical (you choose).

The vertical line represents the closest part of your pattern.

Materials:

Use the SAME materials as the previous experiment (pencil, felt pen, chalk).

Also use the SAME pattern with a vertical line.

Begin:

Show shapes in the pattern using strokes or long narrow marks. .

Try to add light to the pattern using just tonal variation (dark and light).

Keep the shapes simple and broad.

Movement of shapes may be implied.

Then:

Make the foreground dark to a light background (like a fog).

Show light using shape variations.

Rhythm is related to direction.

UNIT 2: Experiment 4

Photocopy or print out the image you used in the previous experiment.

Rule or draw a vertical line across your selected pattern.

The pattern could be either horizontal or vertical (you choose).

The vertical line represents the closest part of your pattern.

Materials:

Use the SAME materials as the previous experiment (pencil, felt pen, chalk).

Also use the SAME pattern with a vertical line.

Begin:

Shade in the pattern using strokes or long narrow marks. .

Then:

Add light to the pattern using just tonal variation (dark and light).

Go from a light foreground to dark background (like night).

Keep the shapes simple and broad.

Use dissimilar tones (black and white) to show some contrast.

UNIT 2: Experiment 5

Photocopy or print out the image you used in the previous experiment.

Rule or draw a vertical line across your selected pattern.

The pattern could be either horizontal or vertical (you choose).

The vertical line represents the closest part of your pattern.

Materials:

Use the SAME materials as the previous experiment (pencil, felt pen, chalk).

Also use the SAME pattern with a vertical line.

Begin:

Shade in the pattern using strokes or long narrow marks.

These indicate a course or movement.

Add light to the pattern using just tonal variation (dark and light).

Then:

Go from a light foreground to dark background (like night).

UNIT 2: Experiment 6

Photocopy or print out the image you used in the previous experiment.

Rule or draw a vertical line across your selected pattern.

The pattern could be either horizontal or vertical (you choose).

The vertical line represents the closest part of your pattern.

Materials:

Use the SAME materials as the previous experiment (pencil, felt pen, chalk).

Also use the SAME pattern with a vertical line.

Begin:

Shade in the pattern using strokes or long narrow marks.

These indicate a course or movement.

Make the shapes dissimilar.

Then:

Add light to the pattern using just tonal variation (dark and light).

Go from a light foreground to dark background (like night).

Major contrast is obvious (black and white).

Minor contrast is where there is little difference (dark grey and brown).

Further thoughts:

If a picture is dark the lightest area will seem to be the most advanced.

This applies even with abstract work.

Thus as light recedes the tones become progressively darker (like at night).

Major contrast is obvious (black and white).

Minor contrast is where there is little difference (dark grey and brown).

Direction relates to a plane or axis, is horizontal, vertical or oblique.

There is a start and an end and can be seen in a serial order or sequence.

There is a link with rhythm and balance.

THIRD Experience Unit:
Use ONE template for a series of explorations of light.

UNIT 3: Experiment 1
Photocopy or print out the image you have chosen.
Modify the size to maintain conformity with your Magic Multiple Miniatures.
Rule or draw a vertical line across your selected pattern.
The pattern could be either horizontal or vertical (you choose).
The line could be ruled straight or drawn freely.
The line could even follow contours created by the shapes in your pattern.
The vertical line represents the closest part of your pattern.
Materials:
Use a coloured material from the previous units. (pencil, felt pen, paint).
Begin:
Create large, small, or somewhere in between shapes.
Keep the shapes simple and broad.
Then:
Vary size of shapes to create a light foreground to dark background (night).

UNIT 3: Experiment 2
Photocopy or print a DIFFERENT pattern than the previous experiment.
Rule or draw a vertical line across your selected pattern.
Modify the size to maintain conformity with your Magic Multiple Miniatures.
The vertical line represents the closest part of your pattern.
Materials:
Use the SAME materials as the previous experiment (pencil, felt pen, chalk).
Begin:
Repeat some shapes.
Use dark and light areas to show form.
Variety may be created by using contrast.
Then:
Use dark foreground to light background (like fog).
Develop a repetition, gradation, alteration, radiation or sequence of marks.

UNIT 3: Experiment 3
Photocopy or print a DIFFERENT pattern than the previous experiment.
Rule or draw a vertical line across your selected pattern.
Modify the size to maintain conformity with your Magic Multiple Miniatures.
The vertical line represents the closest part of your pattern.
Materials:
Use the SAME materials as the previous experiment (pencil, felt pen, chalk).
Begin:
Repeat some shapes.
Use dark and light to show form.
Variety may be created by using contrast.
Imply spaces as well.
Then:
Paint light foreground to dark background (like night).
Develop a repetition, gradation, alteration, radiation or sequence of marks.
Space is the factor that indicates emptiness or a break.

UNIT 3: Experiment 4
Photocopy or print a DIFFERENT pattern than the previous experiment.
Rule or draw a vertical line across your selected pattern.
Modify the size to maintain conformity with your Magic Multiple Miniatures.
The vertical line represents the closest part of your pattern.
Materials:
Use the SAME materials as the previous experiment (pencil, felt pen, chalk).
Begin:
Create simple spheres, cones, cubes, pyramids, prisms, or ovoids.
Balance the shapes about an axis, or radiate them from a point.
There should be an agreement, closeness, relatedness or similarity of parts.
Then:
Work from dark foreground to light background (like fog).
Harmony implies sharing of similar aspects of shape (angular).

UNIT 3: Experiment 5

Photocopy or print a DIFFERENT pattern than the previous experiment.

Rule or draw a vertical line across your selected pattern.

Modify the size to maintain conformity with your Magic Multiple Miniatures.

The vertical line represents the closest part of your pattern.

Materials:

Use the SAME materials as the previous experiment (pencil, felt pen, chalk).

Begin:

Use shapes with soft (blurred) and hard (sharp) edges for modeling light.

The boundary between different shapes is not always sharp or clear cut.

That means at times there should be a soft irregular transition.

Then:

Dark foreground to light background (fog) OR light to dark (night).

UNIT 3: Experiment 6

Photocopy or print a DIFFERENT pattern than the previous experiment.

Rule or draw a vertical line across your selected pattern.

Modify the size to maintain conformity with your Magic Multiple Miniatures.

The vertical line represents the closest part of your pattern.

Materials:

Use the SAME materials as the previous experiment (pencil, felt pen, chalk).

Begin:

Use contrast, radiation, majority area, or repetition of tone.

Emphasis of one aspect at the expense of another creates dominance.

Show shapes with a course of movement.

The movement may be actual or suggested.

Then:

Dark foreground to light background (fog) OR light to dark (night).

Direction links a plane or axis, which may be horizontal, vertical or oblique.

Further thoughts:

Use only ONE (fog/night) tonal light technique in any painting.

Then be consistent throughout the painting.

Some tonal parts may be dominant or subsidiary.

Exact repetition can lead to monotony.

Rhythm is related to direction.

The movement may be actual or implied.

Mass links space (occupy) and may be real (clay) or apparent (drawn).

DEVELOPMENT: Extensions

In the Development extension activities:

Draw on what you have learnt.

You can link what you have learned to your own goals.

DEVELOPMENT: Extension 1
Materials:
Use the SAME materials as used in a previous experiment from Unit One.
Use the SAME pattern as used in a previous experiment Unit One.
Begin:
BUT use only one of the shape light approaches.
Make sure it is consistent throughout the painting.

DEVELOPMENT: Extension 2
Materials:
Use the SAME materials as used in a previous experiment from Unit Two.
Use the SAME pattern as used in a previous experiment Unit Two.
Begin:
Add wholeness by one aspect dominant, or join aspects into a combination,
Make one aspect dominant joining as a combination or enclosing a border.
Use only one of the shape light approaches.

DEVELOPMENT: Extension 3
Materials:
Use the SAME materials as used in a previous experiment from Unit Three.
Use the SAME pattern as used in a previous experiment Unit Three.
Begin:
Use only one of the shape light approaches.

WHERE NEXT:

There are other books that link with this book.
BUT they have a different focus.
The focus is on: Change Processes:

You can specialize by completing ONE of these two books.
Opaque paint (for oils) OR transparent paint (for water-colour)
Completing BOTH books can also be done (for acrylics).
That could even be at different times.

3.1 Opaque Paint to learn to paint in oils.
http://www.amazon.com/dp/B08CPCD827

3.2 Transparent Paint to learn to paint in watercolour.
http://www.amazon.com/dp/B08CP9DK3C

N O T N O W :

Perhaps one of these books could interest you then?

What about your own memories?
YOU could publish them – like I did!
To find out how just get this book.
http://www.amazon.com/dp/B087DWKPTP

Are you a parent, teacher or someone who meets a group regularly?
A simple way to start developing creativity is by displaying things.
To learn exactly how – buy this book.
http://www.amazon.com/dp/B088T1KFQZ

Starting an art career NOW is harder than it ever was.
To learn what to do - download this book.
http://www.amazon.com/dp/B088T7VJ76

Copying is the way most people start to become an artist!
To learn how - download this book.
http://www.amazon.com/dp/B088Y1DPL6

You could be interested in some more of my memories.
Find out what they are - buy this book.
http://www.amazon.com/dp/B088Y4RPL9

SEND TO:

Know anyone interested in chocolate recipes?
Send them a link then.
http://www.amazon.com/dp/B088Y4RPL9

Know anyone interested in THIS book?
http://www.amazon.com/dp/B08CPCBPSW

www.ingramcontent.com/pod-product-compliance
Lightning Source LLC
Chambersburg PA
CBHW030657220526

45463CB00005B/1822